COYOTE ANTHROPOLOGY

COYOTE

ANTHRO-

POLOGY

Roy Wagner

University of Nebraska Press

LINCOLN AND LONDON

Library of Congress Cataloging-in-Publication Data
Wagner, Roy, 1938–
                    Coyote anthropology / Roy Wagner.
p. cm.   ISBN 978-0-8032-1082-0 (cloth : alk. paper)
1. Anthropology—Philosophy. 2. Culture—Philosophy.
3. Culture—Semiotic models. 4. Castaneda, Carlos,
1931–1998—Criticism and interpretation. 5. Coyote
(Legendary character)—Legends. I. Title.
GN33.W283 2010   301.01—dc22   2009053627

Set in Minion Pro by Shirley Thornton
Designed by A. Shahan.

To Graham Richard Everett Wagner

CONTENTS

ILLUSTRATIONS

PROLOGUE

This book and its purpose or effect are based in large part upon an observation I made while teaching a course on the writings of Carlos Castaneda at the University of Virginia. The whole success of Castaneda's work, either in the books or in teaching, depends exclusively on one thing, however else it may be illuminated or obscured by examples: the technique of drawing the sharpest possible contrasts among people, events, or phenomena so that the world as we normally perceive it is thrown into sharp relief, caught in a play of light and shadow between one extreme and another. We could be talking about the *tonal* and the *nagual*; the "recollecting self," as it is called in the text, and the "anticipating self"; about right and wrong, good and evil; between animals and people; between the world of the paleface ("white eyes," as the Apache call him) and the world of the Indian ("first nations," as the Canadians say). But the strategy Castaneda's teachers use is of seriousness and humor. Or, rather—since that is putting it mildly (how often do people talk about "sense of humor"? and when do they ever talk about a "sense of seriousness"?)—a kind of humor that is "off the deep end" on one side, really too funny to be funny at all (rather, world-damaging) and the other, a kind of seriousness that is really super-serious ("critical," as they say) and has very little to do with what we normally mean by this term. Dead-eye seriousness accords best with the kind of exaggeration associated with notions of high respect, extreme humility, taboos, honor and shame, what Don Juan calls "impeccability" and the Marines call Semper Fi, tough love, or just simply "boot camp."

The book you hold in your hands (if you have not by this time discarded it) is one of two I hope to publish on the uses of the Castaneda material in anthropology, each from the standpoint of one of these two appositional points of view. Each of course will use much the same material, and in some cases the same sonnets, but otherwise there will be all the difference in the world between them. This, of course, is the "funny" one, but as we have seen, funny is never really funny until and unless it manages to outrage and overplay its original intent and purpose, tipping the balance it was originally set up to restore. Accordingly I have gone to great lengths to achieve a kind of insouciant Genaro-effect by making use of gross puns, bad jokes, and sonnets and other verses of questionable merit, along with manic expressions of super-serious outrage. I sincerely hope and trust that the reader will indulge me in this.

So of course the funny/serious contrast simply *will not work* in a book of this sort without incurring a good deal of collateral damage. Instead I have substituted a much broader and more useful contrast, between *impersonation* and *expersonation*, to throw the whole subject of anthropology into relief. The secret of everyday values and normal life is just simply that of impersonation—the mimesis that Aristotle talked about. We copy, mimic, and imitate one another every day, in fun *or* in abject seriousness, including our ideas, body movements, and especially our feelings, and have learned to do so since the day we were born, or before. That is the coyote anthropology of everyday life, predatory or not, and also what anthropologists are supposed to be doing in carrying out "participant observation" studies among their subject peoples. We *imitate* the language, thoughts, and lifestyles of other people, copying them as a version of "culture," and this is how the anthropologist is inclined to explain his or her work to the uninitiated Still this is a highly problematic approach, even when fully understood (which is rare). Using one *culture*, if that is the term, to copy or imitate another, or even copying a culture within itself, almost always leads to a sterile and useless tautology—a comparison of comparison with itself.

But, you see, there is another way, best evidenced in what Castaneda's Don Juan (whoever he may be) calls *seeing* and William Shakespeare's play of *Hamlet* addressed in a more traditional way. I call that other way *expersonation* (Don Juan calls it "not-doing"), and in many ways it is the true opposite of anthropology. It works like this: *humor (or anthropology) takes the person out of their perspective, but seeing (expersonation) takes the perspective out of the person.*

"So that's what you meant when you wrote, 'There is no Hamlet quite like Hamlet, not even Hamlet himself.'" Sure, Coyote, Prince Hamlet took the decision to *act himself mad, expersonating* himself by imitating a version of himself that had never existed before, so that by invention if not intention he could speak the truths that no sane Crown Prince would dare utter in a place like Elsinore. But then, after he mistakenly stabbed Polonius (Mr. "To thine own self be true") through the curtain, his decision backlashed on itself. From then on he underwent a complete role reversal: instead of a sane Prince acting himself mad he became a mad invention himself acting sane—a "pretender" in word and deed. Instead of merely *correcting* the situation at court, or calling attention to it, he *obviated* the whole thing. He *expersonated* himself, then tricked Laertes (whose father, Polonius, Hamlet himself had murdered) into *seeing* . . . and took a whole society down in the ancient courtly fashion (I think this means "poison").

"See, Roy, it's all a matter of trance-*parency*."
"Shut up, *cur*."

So what have the "White Eyes" learned, from themselves and from the First Nations? Not much, apparently. Now that traditional North American ethnography has lost most of its credibility to the fleeting enthusiasms of New Age "wannabees" and a plethora of ill-chosen accounts of Indian "Spiritualism," most readers may fail to appreciate the role this kind of extreme exaggeration played in aboriginal Native American social orders. What the early ethnographers called "joking relationships"—an ethic of exaggeration to the point of ridiculousness and over-familiarity and "extreme respect or avoidance relationships" exaggerated to pinnacles of awesomeness and extreme peril—formed a tension that held the whole world of personal interaction within its grasp. Including, and *especially*, one might say, the world of teaching and knowledge. Castaneda did not know what he was getting himself into. Don Juan and Don Genaro do not necessarily *live* this way (though they tell Carlos they do, "like warriors"); they *present* themselves this way.

So it is like the saying the Native Americans have: "Coyote is the best trickster of all, because he *tricks himself*." When you imitate a part of a culture or a person that *cannot be imitated*, that part winds up imitating *you*. (Madness is only a beginning.) And forces are unleashed that no one can comprehend. Reminding one of W. H. Auden's drawing (from "An Unwritten Poem") of the quintessential forger, a man who was able to forge his own signature so poorly that not even the best handwriting experts could tell whether it was an *authentic fake* or one of those cheap imitations one hears so much about these days.

Do you hear me, Coyote?
"I hear you, boss."

ACKNOWLEDGMENTS

Most of us are products of social interactions and meaningful exchanges that have become so much parts of our reality that we could not isolate them even if we tried. The original Coyote anthropologist was Eugene N. Anderson, a much better poet than I, whom I met in Theodore Morrison's composition class at Harvard. Erika, Jonathan, Wendi, and Graham (a native born Texan) help to round out the coyote part of the legacy, as, I suspect, does Carlos Castaneda. On his side of the ledger there are just simply too many, but honor demands that we begin with teachers and colleagues like David M. Schneider, Vic and Edie Turner, Fred Eggan, J. Christopher Crocker, George Mentore, Richard Handler, Gary Dunham, and T. S. Harvey. Then we have the Originals, or creator-heroes of the Castaneda course itself, like Nancy Ammerman Arnest, Douglas Sean Elfers (who made the supreme sacrifice), Matt Edwards, Rob Jackson, the Nagual Andrew Mersen, Aubrey Gilbert, Erika Jacobson, Virginia Busby, Justin Shaffner, Tatiana Tchoudakova, Yana Chertihin, Wairimu Mburathi (plus an attending salient of courageous Kikuyu warriors from Kenya), Kara Frederick, Cameron Suwijn ("The Fast Gun of Yaxchilan"), the Dreaming Nagual Tiffany Luck, Rowan Webster, and Adam Disbrow. The list could go on and on (and it does), but to avoid the contumely of Doug Elfers's favorite appellation for me, "The Nagual Inventory," I need to break off and acknowledge some of the others of the Warriors' Party, Liz Stassinos, Meagan Shaw, Hannah Trible, Tara Thompson, Dawn M. Hayes, Herb Rice, and Yale Landsberg, who have made the Passage Worthwhile.

COYOTE ANTHROPOLOGY

1 | TRICKING MAGIC

The Anthropology of Coyote

There once was a trader, a white man at the store back on the Rez, who was so good at tricking Indians they were a little bit proud of him. One day an Indian came up to the counter and said to the trader, "Now you are the cheatin' wonder of the whole civilized world, but that one over there, he's even better than you are."

"Why him? He's only a scrawny critter!"

"Yep, that's the one. So why don't you let him prove it?"

So the white man ambled over to Coyote and said, "Let's you and me have us a tricking contest and see who is the better cheater."

"Won't work," said *canis latrans*, "'cause I left my tricking magic back home, and that's two days away."

"No problem," said *homo not exactly sapiens*, "because I can lend you my hoss, and you can go and fetch your magic quicker'n a Noo Yawk minute."

"No way," said the candid canid, "because I am basically a predator, and all your nag's got to do is snuff my scent, and he'll buck me off in a *Lubbock nanosecond*."

"Well, dawgnabbit," said the trader, "I'll just lend you my *clothes*, too, and when the hoss takes a whiff of the scent, it'll snuff *me* instead of *you*."

Now that is just exactly what happened, dawgnabbit and all; Coyote took the trader's hoss, put on his clothes, and *blithely* rode away.

Coyote: "Now, see, Roy, that just goes to show."
Roy: "Goes to show what?"

Coyote: "Perception is a very tricky thing."

Roy: "Not half so tricky as *representation*; for anything you see in these lines, you're gonna see because I *represented* it that way."

Coyote: "I wouldn't be too sure about that; there's always a trick involved, and, like your Barok friends told you in New Ireland, once you realize that something is a fake . . ."

Roy: "Or maybe that *everything* is a fake . . ."

Coyote: "You stand, not at the end of knowledge, but at its beginning."

Roy: "And now you're gonna tell me that you left your tricking magic back home."

Coyote: "Not exactly. I got it right here with me. Look in a mirror."

Roy: "So why is perception a fake?"

Coyote: "See, Roy, we do not see the world we see, hear the sounds we hear, touch the things we touch, or in any way perceive what we perceive, but that something else comes in-between."

Roy: "Now what is this, some kind of sly canid Plato's Cave analogy? Like you canids have a flight-or-fight response inhibitor at the back of your brain?"

Coyote: "Hey, Roy, I got one right in front of me. Besides, what *is* a brain besides a flight-or-fight response inhibitor?"

Roy: "Well, then, so is the whole neural net of the body, autonomic as well as sympathetic, since what we deign to call an *organism* or *body* is in that sense the flip side of the brain, how it really works, and its basic intelligence-network."

Coyote: "*You* talk to *me* and 'flip,' eh? It's more like *counter*intelligence; the brain is the only organ in the body that is narcissistic enough to actually *believe* it is thinking. That is why we coyotes have such small ones."

Roy: "I get it; *you're* the 'something else' that comes in-between?"

Coyote: "Sure 'nuff, pardner; I always come in-between—between myself and everything else. I *have* to trick myself in order to trick anyone else. I am exactly what *perception* would be if it knew enough about itself to *represent* itself accordingly."

Roy: "Like what we perceive is actually our *thinking* about perception?"

Coyote: "Good guess, though the truth is actually more scary than that."

Roy: "Thus if *thinking* really amounts to perceiving oneself to be perceiving thought itself, then what we do every time we perceive is to perceive the act of perception, or, in other words, *represent* the seen to the seer. We never *see* the light at all . . ."

Coyote: "But that the light sees itself as us, for *what* we see and *how* we see are one and the same thing."

Roy: "We do not perceive but that we perceive the act of perception, a perception that *represents* itself to be the seen."

Coyote: "See? I always knew you had a little bit of coyote in you. When you see the light of a star what you are actually seeing is the impulse that your optic nerve makes of it, like a dawg star, or, in other words, *you can't be Sirius*. There is always a *paws* in between."

Roy: "Like time-lapse photography, eh?"

Coyote: "Or time-lapse acoustics, in the case of the ear, that listens for itself. Or time-lapse tactility, in the case of the skin and motion-sensors. Or even time-lapse cognition in the case of the brain."

Roy: "Don't look now, but you're on *candid camera*."

Coyote: "In each case we perceive the reflexive interval of the work, or energy, that the body uses to make sense of the world, and thus of itself. We are always *one step behind* the action that is really out there, which we know by reflex alone. And for the same reason. Which is not very *rational* at all. We are always one step behind that action itself, which is *in here*, and even in our thinking about what is in here."

Roy: "Wow, that really *is* scary, for even to think about being one step behind we have to take a step behind that thinking, and then step backward to know even that. It is as though the whole course of perception, and therefore *memory*, runs backward to the action of what we think we are doing."

Coyote: "Back to the very beginning, like effects causing their own causes *every single time*. Like we can only know the world of perception *in reverse to ourselves*, and moving forward in time is like the illusion that memory needs in order to confront itself?"

Roy: "How else would the memory remember *what* to remember, or even *how* to remember? Like we have to *think ourselves up* again, come out of the dream world every time we get up in the morning, re-anticipating the past in order to extend it into the future. Like, 'Let's see; where was I yesterday so I can get on with today?'"

Coyote: "Like 'I left my tricking magic back home, and now I have to go home and get it.' For there would be no 'today' without that tricking magic. Or like what they call the 'bubble of reflection' in Castaneda's books: the idea that that 'something else in-between' surrounds us like an opaque bubble so that all we can see and know of the world is our own image or imagery reflected back to us by the inside surface of the bubble."

Roy: "Or like Wittgenstein's observation in the *Tractatus*, that 'What is reflected in language cannot be said by means of language.'"

Coyote: "Case in point, Roy, since Wittgenstein himself was obliged to state *in language* the fact that *what he had stated*—the proposition itself—cannot be stated in language. That guy has *coyote possibilities*; too bad he had to assume a human form."

Roy: "That might be debated, Coyote, for by this time all we have left of him is a set of *reflections* upon language, give or take the fact that that's about all that language is."

Coyote: "By *his* standards, not mine. But didn't he also say, later in the *Tractatus*, that 'the meanings of this world must lie outside of this world?' He actually drew a diagram to show what he meant, illustrating that the eye is never included in its own field of vision. Which would have to mean that *meaning* itself is far from the purely subjective quality that the bubble of perception makes it out to be, forcing us to perceive our own perceptions, and that the eye *does* see through the bubble of reflection every single time only to be arrested later by the time-lapse of thinking about it."

Roy: "In other words, we see what we know but do not really know what we see, given that the meanings are real enough but the *meanings of those meanings* are not, given that we falsify them in the process of self-reflection."

Coyote: "And so Wittgenstein was a real coyote after all, and the bubble of reflection is the subject of its own illusionism and far too simple a device even for the purposes for which Don Juan had intended it. Reflection, one way or another, is its own worst enemy."

Roy: "You mean like my own best observation about mirrors, that 'the One in the mirror steals your own act of perception—looking and thinking—but only to see and know itself.'"

Coyote: "Well, that too; your 'One in the mirror' is actually what Don Juan would call an 'ally,' like most of your girlfriends. But what I really mean is that the so-called bubble of reflection is more properly figured as a visual *chiasmus*, the type of statement or relation that has an *impasse* within it, which turns out to mean more than the statement itself. Like the epigrams of Heraclitus: 'We live the gods' deaths, and they live ours.' The same words are used twice, but with a different *twist*, or intent, each time."

Roy: "I get it, like 'the One in the mirror steals your act of perception, looking through *your* eyes, but only because you, looking through *her* eyes, have stolen hers.' Sounds like the story of my life, or what really goes on in sex, or *chained orgasm*, or the life of Sigmund Freud (*unexpurgated edition*)."

Coyote: "Or Wittgenstein's, as reflected in the aphorism of his fellow Viennese, Karl Kraus: 'An aphorism is either half-true or one-and-a-half-times-true.' The eye that sees right through the bubble of reflection gets more truth, or meaning, *than it can make sense of* (this is what Don Juan calls *seeing*, or unmediated perception) *because* the action of making sense, or perceiving the perception, reflects itself in the process of doing so, and only lets a fraction of that meaning filter through."

Roy: "Now I get it *all over again*: a woman who can chain her orgasm is actually *riding on her own climaxes*, with little or no help from her friends."

1. (above) *Message in a Bottle #1: Mobius Surface as an Outward Rotation of a Klein Bottle*

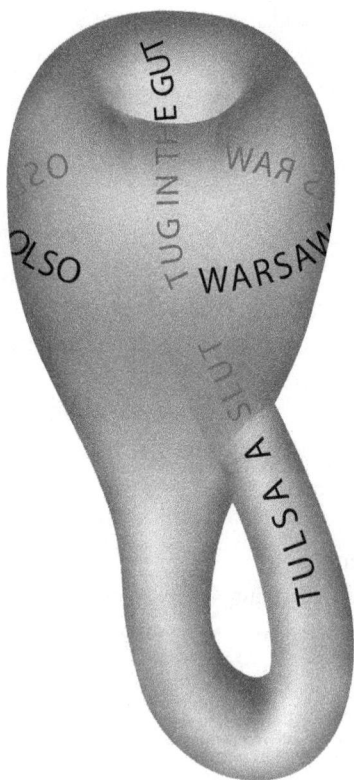

2. (below) *Message in a Bottle #2: Klein Surface as an Inward Rotation of a Mobius*

Coyote: "Like that damn fool trader I left back there, missing his mount and buckass naked. Beware of allies, Roy, and false conclusions; *these are not the conclusions you should be drawing.* Not even in the dirt."

Roy: "Okay pal. So what *is* the true shape of the bubble of reflection?"

Coyote: "A Klein bottle, or what the topologists would call a Klein-surface.

Coyote: You are perhaps familiar with what is called a Mobius strip: a strip of paper twisted through 180 degrees in the middle and then joined, end to end, so that the resultant figure has only one side and one edge (fig. 1, the Mobius Strip Search). It is actually a three-dimensional figure closed upon itself in one of its dimensions."

Roy: "Like most of my love affairs.

Coyote: "Yeah, Roy. Sure, Roy. 'Of all the cheap gin joints . . . etc., etc., she had to *figure* in mine.' Too bad you didn't have more *edge*."

Roy: "Well, at least I had a 180-degree *twist* in the middle. So what is a Klein bottle?"

Coyote: "It's like a 3D *elevation* of your love life, or a chiasmus reflected again within itself, or, strictly speaking, a three-dimensional figure closed down upon itself in two of its dimensions: a single surface that is at the same time both inside and outside of itself (see fig. 2)."

Roy: "So seeing out of it *is* seeing into it, and vice-versa; what it unites is what it separates, and what it separates is what it unites—exactly like language, in Wittgenstein's perspective, both inside and outside of meaning all at once. Where *do* you find gals like that, Coyote?"

Coyote: "Believe me, *they* come looking for *me*. But as for your observation, it *is* Wittgenstein's perspective, not Don Juan's. For what is reflected in language is precisely what cannot be said in it or in another metaphor, which is unglossable in lexical terms. So what is reflected *as* metaphor, the meaning that is otherwise invisible and unqualifiable must necessarily lie outside the world of language."

Roy: "Like saying that metaphor is language's way of trying to figure out what we mean by it."

Coyote: "Or else like learning that we do not learn language at all, but instead actually *teach ourselves to it*. For in both cases we must do something that we are not normally allowed to do, which is to treat language as though it had a mind or intelligence of its own, that is, to grant it an *agency* in its own right.

Roy: "Isn't that what linguists do, in a purely hypothetical sense? And isn't it what Heisenberg did when he called our inability to determine both the location and the velocity of a particle at the same time an *uncertainty principle*, as though the particle itself were uncertain as to its own motion and location?"

Coyote: "And isn't that what you are doing to me right now by *anthropomorphizing* me, pretending that I am an anthropologist just like you? Heisenberg pointed out that we *interfere* with tiny particles in the very act of observing them, and so re-project our own intentions inadvertently upon the particle (or Coyote, as the case may be). But what he did not allow himself to concede was that the particle was doing the same thing back to him, for 'it' had entered his own thought process as though it were part of his own neural net."

Roy: "Which, by that time, it *was*. Or, in other words, by virtue of the funda*mental* subject/object shift, *I got coyotes on the brain*."

Coyote: "Or whatever may be left of it by this time."

Roy: "And that's how you manage to pick up these fancy gals, or tricky chicks, or *aporetic fantasy women*, as the ancient Greeks might have called them. Self-symmetries, and nothing else; for stripped bare and held up for all the world to see, the Mobius is really only the symmetry of *space to itself*, whereas the Klein surface is the self-symmetry of *time* with respect to space. Show a little *respect*, Coyote; look again at those *figures*."

Coyote: "Well, it's true that we coyotes get it on by *moonlight*, and that the *visual* is a trap that has caught better mathematicians than you and me. But you oughtta see what these gals can do when they strut their stuff."

Roy: "*What* stuff; *crack*? Or maybe booze? I'm talkin' the basic subject/ object shift. The Klein is an alcoholic, like a gyro with no scope; can't climb out of the bottle without falling back in again—poor gal, never even notices her own *retort*."

Coyote: "Sure, and by the *deference* between them, the Mobius is the ultimate 'cocktail personality'—a cute little trick, decidedly superficial, with delicious curves, little substance, a bad case of mono, and practically no edge."

Roy: "Like I said, my own love life come back to haunt me."

Coyote: "And *that's* the big trouble with you anthropologists, isn't it? You want to be the figure as well as the ground and invest immense amounts of your personal experience in highly obsessive encounters with alien points of view so that you get to *be* the subject/object shift instead of only talking about it. So that, as you put it, you can get to know your *own* culture—whatever the hell *that* might be—by knowing intimately all the ways you can*not* be whatever it was you were supposed to be in the first place. Which, by this time, is *up for grabs*."

Roy (perspiring): "Gee whiz, at least we get a culture for our very own."

Coyote: "Oh yeah? *Which* culture, the one you don't know so well that by this time you know it by heart, or the other one that you pretend to have been born into?"

Roy: "Hey, gimme a break; my craft, or sullen art, is simply a matter of what Don Juan calls 'not-doing.'"

Coyote: "I'm not finished, and I'm not done talking. By this time in the game the process has become irreversible; you have become basically *dyslexic* about the comparative method itself, and cannot tell your own private *subjective* experiences—your 'love life,' et cetera—from the generic human ones that you pretend to call 'objective' . . .

Roy: " . . . Awwwwww . . . "

Coyote: " . . . . and as it comes to *fundamentals*, subject/object shifts, and all, you remind me of what you said about the *post-*

modernists, or hermeneutic 'self-interpretation' freaks, the bane of *everyone's* existence. You said, and I quote, 'They have their heads shoved so far up their own *fundaments* they can see light between their own teeth.' End of quote."

Roy: AND end of Coyote by the way, now that you've finished talking. And also the end of *phenomenology*, or whatever it is they call themselves—I call it 'lockjaw.' As for you, Nomme du Chien, what you do not know about not-doing could fit in the palm of anyone's hand, even if it was not occupied by *something else*."

Coyote: "I think you just tipped *yours*, Roy, Nomme du Louis Quatorz. So what is this not-doing about which we have, by now, heard so much."

Roy: "Not-doing is *the way of the warrior*, a power so awesome, as Don Juan himself put it, that no one who is not a *maven* at the art, a Man of Knowledge, should even breathe the name of it."

Coyote: "Gee, whiz, I'm positively *breathless*."

Roy: "Good thing, too, at least in *first attention*, which goes immediately to the *perception* we have been talking about. The outlined *figures* of people, places, and things that you have been trained to look for and think about (so that by now it has become quite unconscious) are the *first attention reality* of your world. The *background* of those figures, which you notice only in passing, is *second-attention reality*."

Coyote: "Sure. As they say: 'figures don't lie, but liars can figure.'"

Roy: "The sounds and shapes that you have been trained to react to and project (so that by now it has become quite unconscious) form the pattern or content of first-attention reality. The spaces between and around those words, or between the words and the things they stand for, which you notice only in passing, form the backdrop of second-attention reality."

Coyote: "Gotcha. See, I'm a *quick study*. The figures or words depend on the backgrounds or spaces, just as the backgrounds or spaces depend on *them*, so that first attention and second attention are locked into a mutual dependency with one another. There is, in other words, a *normally invisible* and *conventionally*

inaudible FIGURE GROUND REVERSAL, a potential INVER-
SION of the foreground and background attentions that is always at work, and at play, between them. And that interplay or
interference patterning is *the key to all perception, all humor and
seriousness*; it is the key to POWER, the hinge of *seeing*, and the
essence of all decisions that we can make, or even unmake."

Roy (perspiring): "By so much is this the case (as Wittgenstein
said 'The world is all that is the case') and also *not* the case: that
the actual *experiencing* of the two attentions at one and the same
time, what Don Juan calls the *third attention*, is not something
one can have without *dying* in the process. The Yucatec Mayans
made an image of this, showing the *immortal symmetry of symmetry with* itself in the form of the moth and the butterfly—life
forms that incorporate the totality of transformation within
the lifecycle—turning into one another. They called that image
Hunab Ku, which means 'The One and Only God.'

Coyote: "And I would call it 'No More Butterfly Collecting, or, The
One Anthropologist Who Actually Made It.' No offense to your
love life."

Roy: "None taken. Though you should have seen Nancy."

Coyote: "But that key can only be used to unlock the worlds of
power, perception, humor, and seriousness WHEN USED DE-
LIBERATELY (this means directly and *on purpose*, in a fully
conscious way), and, when not used in that way is only a potential. Don Juan calls the deliberate and direct use of this potential, implicit in everything we know and do, NOT-DOING. The
technique, or insight, or art of this is very risky and dangerous
but also very liberating. For when used consistently, or when it
becomes a habit, IT CAN TAKE ON A LIFE OF ITS OWN.
The warrior must be very self-disciplined, and the warrior's
heart must be fortified to stand *competition with it*. Don Genaro
does so every time he enters the edge of his power, which is the
essence of humor itself; DON GENARO IS A SHAMAN OF
THE FIGURE-GROUND REVERSAL. A crazy person is one
who cannot stand the competition; the key unlocks the person's
sanity instead."

Roy (marveling): "You're a *long way* from Texas, son!"

Coyote: "All inventions are not-doings of some technique that existed beforehand. (Example: a piston engine contains the explosion within its mechanism; a jet engine contains the mechanism within the explosion.) All insights are not-doings of some perspective that existed beforehand—here's where you anthropologists get your payoff . . . "

Roy: " . . . or alimony, as the case may be . . . "

Coyote: " . . . as are all jokes (a joke contains the key within the lock, and then the lock within the key, or punch line)."

Roy: "When the technique, or invention, or insight of NOT-DOING is used directly, deliberately, and purposefully to unlock THE WHOLE WORLD OF PERCEPTION AND EXPERIENCE, in whatever way this may be accomplished, then that world takes on a NOT-DOING life of its own, and *your* world *stops*. Don Juan calls this STOPPING THE WORLD. Then coyotes talk to you, and dung beetles roll the world away. After that nothing is the same anymore, even though everything reverts to normal."

Coyote: "Talk to *me* about 'normal,' hey? Don Juan and Don Genaro use this technique at first to make Carlos's car disappear from his world ("Sorry, guy, it's all in your *perspective*), lock his view of things within him (the car lost *him*; he didn't lose the car), then laugh themselves silly to watch him riding on air, deliberately working the gears and thinking he is driving a real car. And then, somewhat later, when all of this had sunk in: 'Big deal, you stopped the world!' It is too *simple* for most of us to do."

Roy: "In my case it was *hummingbird* who stopped my world."

Coyote: "What? And not Nancy? Boy, I am surprised at you."

Roy: "Well, *she tried*, and sometimes it takes a long time to stop the world."

Coyote: "Say, isn't your definition of humor 'getting the point by not getting it?'"

Roy: "Also my definition of *divorce*."

Coyote: "You *gotta* do better than that."

Roy: "Humor or irony, whatever else they might mean or be, are the core or basis of any attempt at explanation; the explanation of a joke, always a mistake, is another version of the joke of explanation itself. And this, for the fact that irony itself, is simply the inversion of what we normally consider to be *cause* or *agency* in that it gives one the effect first and then offers a wry suggestion as to what the *cause* may or may not have been."

Coyote: "Roy, didn't you yourself write (2005: 233) that 'Cause-and-effect depends, for its very usefulness or 'predictive' efficacy, upon a purely arbitrary distinction or division imposed upon a unitary action so as to project the *working illusion* that one part of it is anterior (causal) or antecedent to the other.'"

Roy: "Sure did, but after that (loc. cit.) I also wrote: 'What we have in the normal interplay between the humorous and the agentive—the fact that jokes on one hand and inventions on the other seem to have no easily established or fixable point of origination and seem to arise of their own accord—is a figure-ground reversal that controls the realm of thought and action instead of being controlled by it.'"

Coyote: "And that would be your subject/object shift—the joke of invention and the invention of the joke—so that Don Juan and Don Genaro inverted the order of cause and effect to disappear Carlos's car."

Roy: "Then the car would have disappeared *them*, wouldn't it? Actually, the figure-ground reversal is all-important to our grasp of humor as well as agency, and Don Juan simply took the fact that both are out of our direct control—jokes as well as inventions appearing out of nowhere—and inverted it upon ourselves."

Coyote: "Like 'why do you need magic when you already have it,' eh? Look, Roy, unless you can tell me how this was done, or how humor *is* dependent on figure-ground reversal, we might as well dismiss the whole thing as a fraud or an illusion."

Roy: "But I *was* a fraud and an illusion, no more and no less so than cause and effect itself, or, for that matter, human perception."

Coyote: "Come again?"

The Explanation of Humor and the Humor of Explanation

Roy: "Don Juan says 'it is possible to *feel* with the eyes.' We have learned, and we are taught, to look as we think and think as we look, to pick out *figures* in the world, figures that correspond to our thoughts and our words for things. But at the same time our eyes are also *feeling* the background, the 'ground' or field of the shapes and figures that we *look* for ourselves *into* the world around us. Don Juan calls the work that we do in thinking as we look and looking as we think 'first-attention,' and the work that we do in feeling the background with our eyes 'second-attention.' Second-attention is our 'dream' of the world and our bodies use this feeling of the world to move with."

Coyote: "So then the whole axis between *thinking* and *being* is controlled by the figure-ground reversal of the two attentions, or foreground and background, and Descartes could have said 'I am, therefore I think.'"

Roy: "*Sum vel cogito*, Coyote. It's an either/or proposition, a zero-sum game. Humor depends on its 'funny edge' to make us laugh, and that is why cartoons or 'pictures in the head' of the humorous situation are important to it. "Funny' is where looking and thinking loses it, and the funny edge, or 'far side,' is a crack between the worlds of looking and feeling, a place where feeling breaks through the focus that looking and thinking made for it and focuses *us* instead. The *body* laughs. The mind only thinks about laughing, but then gives up and turns it into an explanation instead."

Coyote: "Descartes never had it so good, or so *bad*, either; the *worst* jokes of all are always the very best."

Roy: "It gets even better. As Matt Edwards once put it, in my Castaneda class, 'Humor is the *close knowledge* of *anything.* Plus or minus the Cartesian coordinates.'"

Coyote: "*Anything* at all, any fact or situation in the world of looking and thinking could be made funny if it were focused in the right way, so it is the humorist's job to make the particular joke or cartoon seem trivial or unimportant, *disqualify* it, so as to save the moral importance of looking and thinking."

Roy: "Or, in other words, *never put Descartes before a horse of a different color*, which is actually a *species* of what Don Juan calls 'controlled folly.' *We* laugh to control the folly of actually *seeing* through the folly of our normal interpretation, closing upon a 'knowledge' of things, which is actually *forbidden* to the shapes and figures we make in looking and thinking. Don Juan laughs to control the folly of looking and thinking. There is all the difference in the world between those two perspectives, yet neither of them really belongs to the commonsense world."

Coyote: "So then what Don Juan calls *seeing* would be like looking *through* humor rather than looking directly *at* it, the way we do in the 'setup,' or opening scenario of a joke."

Roy: "To *see*, in Don Juan's sense, it would be necessary to isolate the ability to feel with the eyes, bring it up through the whole feeling and moving potential of the body, and use it to break the focus of the looking and thinking world. The 'funny edge' done backward, and upside-down (Genaro tries to do this with his acrobatics, and his laughing at Carlos); *nothing* would be funny anymore, but nothing would be *serious* either I (c.f. Don Juan: 'in *seeing* all things go to nothing'). It is a lot easier to talk or think about this than to actually *do*, because the looking and thinking part of us always gets grabbed by the work it was trained to do."

Coyote: "So then *seeing* could make a car disappear."

Roy: "Along with everything else, including all the *referentials*, or coordinate systems, that allow one to determine whether the car, or anything else, is either *there* or *not there*."

Coyote: "So, then, and correct me if I'm wrong: it would not be *po-litically correct* to make such a determination at all, or even use the works of Castaneda, since the whole rationale of political correctness stems from *a total lack of standards, or criteria, for making judgments about things*."

Roy: "Well, then I will have to correct you, if only for *political* reasons, since you are *wrong*. Political correctness is actually a form of *overcompensation* for the lack of standards or criteria; it consists in the art of making exaggerated, overdetermined judgments about the most trivial matters—the more trivial, the better."

Coyote: "In that case acute, perceptual judgment, or even *seeing*, are like the aphorism Karl Kraus talked about: they are either half true or one-and-a-half times true. Or like the special, coded *language*, called 'anthrospeak,' which anthropologists have developed in order to communicate with one another."

Roy: "Sure. Either they *see* and can't talk about it, or else they talk about it and can't see beyond their own profession. Most of what Don Juan calls *doing* actually works by not-doing, whereas most of what he calls *not-doing* is actually a secret form of *doing*. Clear?"

Coyote: "As *mud*. Anthropologists have a sense of humor about everything but themselves."

Roy: "*Wrong again*, Coyote. They have a sense of humor *only* about themselves, since they don't take anyone else *seriously* enough, or else they take them *too* seriously. Most anthropological *theory* (forget *practice*—there isn't any) works by getting itself wrong and then trying to get itself right about why it was wrong in the first place. It is a clear case of what someone once called 'a working misunderstanding.'"

Coyote: "*Who* called it a working misunderstanding?"

Roy: "*I* always thought it was Marshall Sahlins, but then Marshall said it was me, and then Jim Bohannan said that both of us got it from him."

Coyote: "So who was right?"

Roy: "That's the point, see? It's like what Robert Murphy called 'Schneider's Law,' which is actually the not-doing of what most people call Murphy's Law, since Murphy got tired of hearing his name taken in vain. You know about Murphy's Law, don't you?"

Coyote: "No."

Roy: "Good. The 'not-doing' or working misunderstanding of Murphy's Law is Schneider's Law. Very cutting and tailored to fit."

Coyote: "Tailored to fit what?"

Roy: "Why, *itself*, of course—nobody said these guys were sloppy. Schneider's Law, according to Murphy, is that 'Everything in structural-functional theory reduces to the simple proposition that *if things didn't work in the way that they actually do, they would work in some other way.*'

Coyote: "So what is Murphy's Law, according to Schneider?"

Roy: "*If anything can go wrong, it probably will*, or, in other words, the not-doing of the very same thing."

Coyote: "What thing?"

Roy: "The fabulous *Ding an Sich*, or 'thing in and of itself' (e.g., *figure* alone, without its ground), much celebrated in Teutonic folklore and pseudophilosophy (read: 'phenomenology') until clarified by Wittgenstein in his brilliant proposition, '*We picture facts to ourselves.*'"

Coyote: "Apply a) Murphy's Law, and then b) Schneider's Law to Wittgenstein's proposition to find out what the *Ding an Sich* really means."

Roy: "a) *If anything could possibly go wrong in phenomenology it certainly already has*, and b) *If we did not picture facts to ourselves then facts would picture us to them*, and thus by the very nature of *figure-ground reversal the subject/object shift* that is necessary to picture the fact in the first place, and, last but not least, Don Juan's *seeing* and the ancient Mayan *Hunab Ku* (viz., Was it I dreaming I was a butterfly, or was it a butterfly dreaming it was me?)"

Coyote: "So what is Wagner's Law?"

Roy: "Wagner's Law, which I thought up all by myself when I was about ten years old, is: *Of all the possible things that could happen in the next moment, only one of them will.*"

Coyote: "And where did Wagner's Law come from?"

Roy: "The next moment."

Coyote: "And what is Wagner's *practice*, as opposed to Wagner's Law?"

Roy: "Wagner's practice *is*, logically, *opposed* to Wagner's Law, if only to save the plurality or plenitude of the world's event-structure or inventory from further attenuation and obloquy. It is, in other words—(and a whole lot of them, too)—to continually revisit the past, recapitulate the past, even *regurgitate* the past, in search of even more concrete examples of what everybody already knows abstractly to be true, which is that anthropology is nothing without its *digressions*."

Coyote: "And this has the effect of . . . "

Roy: "Contrition. Pizzazz. Human interest value. Suave demonstrative facility. But, most of all, humor, since, as we have seen, humor is the *sine qua non* of explanatory prowess, even in its smaller version, the *prowette*. Furthermore, every visible or audible reaction to humor, regardless of intent, has the effect of a regurgitative impulse, or threat-gesture, from the risus, or grin, to the belly laugh. Even the sound of laughter, like *ha ha* or *ho ho*, is like a backward speech event, for it models the word upon the *breath* rather than the breath upon the word."

Coyote: "Thus the effect of Wagner's practice is to do everything possible to keep us from getting to that thoroughly predictable *next moment*, or, in other words, to keep us from finding out how they made Carlos's car disappear."

Roy: "Oh *that*. Well, see, that is a matter of Don Juan's practice, or what he calls 'sorcery,' and what you or I might prefer to call an interplay between memory and chance: *nonfortuitous happenstance*."

Coyote: "Aren't memory and chance *opposites* of one another?"

Roy: "Yes and no; they are opposites that both attract and repel at the same time."

Coyote: "Then what is the *relation* between them? How does the control of future event ('prediction') stand with respect to past recollection ('deduction,' 'afterthought,' 'pragmatic afterlife')? What are the *chances* of their mutual integration in the human actor or thinker? By what deductive process might they be opposites? If there is a point of mutual confusion between them, a sort of *humor* of the afterthought, how might that humor be manipulated to advantage, as in a joke? How *will* one remember something in the future, and how will that postponed recollection be reconciled with a present intention to do so?"

Roy: "We're really full of ourselves today, aren't we? 'How shall I go about remembering today tomorrow?' If intention and memory *share the same description*, a conclusion that is a virtual 'no brainer' (all that we know, including the language by which we know it, must be *remembered*, and so all that we *intend* to know will be some recombination of that memory)."

Coyote: "I see what Don Juan means by 'sorcery.' The real 'brainer,' or Sorcery, is not how and why intention and memory work on the same basic experiential corpus ('description') but rather how we manage to separate the two in order to locate *ourselves*, interpolate the position ('now,' 'the present') that we all seem to share right here in the MIDDLE OF TIME."

Roy: "Wow, Coyote, you're really good; what did you do, just kill a *sheep* or something?"

Coyote: "A clue to this manipulation is given by the ancient Roman *Ars Memoria*, the 'Art of Memory' used by the famous orators of the Roman Senate and law courts. Cicero did it this way: you pick an edifice, like your house, that is very familiar to you—you know the layout and the rooms by habit (it is a memory-place, or *placed* memory), you know the details of each room, the furniture, objects, details of the objects, and the habit-structures that go with them. You *made* them all, and you should *know from yourself*."

Roy: "Then, as I recall, you place all the details of what you want to say (e.g., *will remember*) in your speech or oration *in one-to-one-correspondence* with the details of the edifice and its objects. When you say your piece, the motion of your progress through the memory-chamber *becomes* the ordering of your speech; you *walk your mind* through the building, and nothing is left to chance. That was the ancient Roman *recapitulation* (and no wonder Rome fell)."

Coyote: "I get your drift—did the *Ars Memoria* teach the Romans how to think? Sure, but *only of themselves*. Enforced habit, it turns out, is a *real killer*, and "memory" is only the tip of the iceberg. Now we still have most of the buildings that "remembered" the Romans, though the people themselves are all gone."

Roy: "But the epistemological implications of this are prodigious:

what we have in the *Ars Memoria* is the re-invention of the Roman Empire as a self-decomposing process. It is *absolutely foolproof.* For if the thing we call 'memory' were really *structured* in that way, the *art* of memory would only serve to make that fact more explicit. And if the memory were *not* structured in that way, you would still come out ahead, for you would have invented it on your own. It is at one and the same time what Don Juan calls 'stopping the world' and what I call 'the invention of culture.'"

Coyote: "And what *I* would call *stopping the digression.* You are very famous for your digressions, aren't you, Roy?"

Roy: "Sure, Coyote, and you for your *re*-gressions. And Don Juan for his trance-gressions, shaman though he may have been. 'Stopping the world,' as Don Juan knows it, is really only *stopping the description of the world as we know it,* that is, erasing the *lexical referentials* or 'familiars' (personal history, etc.) by which we know the things that we do know from the metaphors that take off from them."

Coyote: "Sorcery survives in the human race not because it is the *accused* but because it is the *accuser.* Tell *that* to your Roman courts. That is the simple structure of all of Don Juan's arguments, and all of his conclusions. He uses a simple memory/intention trick, or subject/object shift, a *sleight-of-mind* on Carlos every time he needs to *show him something real,* and I prefer to call that trick *the Gimmick.* You may call it anything you will, but please be aware when it is being done to you."

Roy: "Does that mean that this book is a version of the Gimmick?"

Coyote: "*Asked and answered,* Roy: you should know from yourself."

Roy: "Since it 'works' by switching the very evidentials, or self-descriptive referentials, that 'working' itself uses to fix the parameters of its own subjectivity or objectivity, telling itself from itself, as it were, what evidence do we have that 'it' is aware of what it is doing?"

Coyote: "What do you mean by 'it,' Roy, this book, or Don Juan's sorcery, or the Gimmick of the subject/object shift?"

Roy: "Asked and answered, Coyote; that's *it*. The *point*, I mean: *of all the possible things that could happen in the next moment, only one of them will*. Everything we think and know about the world *goes back into itself*, for that is the basic recapitulative strategy of *knowing, thinking, and memory*. But the *next thing to happen* may be pure chance, for all we know."

Coyote: "To answer your original question, about whether 'it' is aware of itself, we have all the evidence in the world that Don Juan and Don Genaro knew exactly what they were 'doing' when they made the car disappear, which was in fact *not doing*. But we have no evidence whatsoever that "it," or *not doing*, ever knows what it is really doing, since its basic job is to erase its own evidence."

Roy: "So it all goes back to the manipulation of memory and chance, eh?"

Coyote: "Sure, 'back engineering,' as they call it in the UFO trade."

Back Engineering: How They Disappeared the Car

Roy: "In *A Separate Reality* Don Juan showed Carlos the same leaf falling from the same sycamore tree several times over, as though it were a single event replayed in a movie of itself. (How many times, in our histories, did Caesar fall in the Forum?) But the *piece de resistance* took place in *Journey to Ixtlan*, when Don Juan and Don Genaro 'made Carlos's car disappear,' caused him to re-invent (remember') it, and then laughed themselves silly to see him riding on thin air, in a seated position actually scudding over the ground, working an invisible gearshift and clutch pedals, *objects*, as it were."

Coyote: "Carlos said that every time they did something like this, he himself lost track of the passage of time."

Roy: "And he himself is the only source of our information about this, isn't he?"

Coyote: "For all we would know that, too, was like watching a movie of itself; what actually took place during the 'filming' of it was as much beside the point of what was depicted in the film as the Gimmick of the traditional Hindu 'rope trick' is to what the spectators remember about it. The surprising thing is that the play of illusion in these quasi-events can also be recovered from the illusion itself, provided one knows *where to look*. If Don Juan's illusionary tactics were staged (as in the traditional rope trick) through the subliminal redeployment of moving objects and human perception in relation to one another, as in a movie itself."

Roy: "Back engineering; *object* lesson. One must *see through* the illusionism of the movie to realize that the tank-treads or wheel-spokes in the film run backward to the motion of the tank or wagon itself, and *not by accident* either. For the very same illusion is responsible for the illusion—really a 'movie' of time—that is projected in the wheel clock's 'measurement' of time, in that the rocker-arm of the escapement mechanism catches the sprockets of the drive-wheel at *successively previous* moments of its rotation. Time, as it were, must not only pass, but actually pass itself up."

Coyote: "Or *off*, like the actor it is. 'Seeing through' the falsified subjectivity in the case of the disappearing car, one can reach the following (startling) conclusion: *Carlos did not really lose his car until he found it, and did not really find his car until he 'lost it.'* This derives automatically from the conclusions reviewed above: that memory, like thought itself, goes backwards in time, but the illusion of temporal progression comes forward through the retrospection of cognition (sort of like the eye seeing nothing but its own energy). But to check this out, we need to go back to the beginning of the narrated event, and then follow through."

Roy: "This is the double vision, both times at once, of past-in-its-own-future and future-in-its-own-past. After announcing what they are about to do, Don Juan and Don Genaro take Carlos to the place in the desert where he had left his car (locked, in fact, so that no one could steal it). They flank Carlos from the front, acting strangely and make absurd batting motions with their arms, either to distract Carlos or to bat the (normally invisible—but hell, no one can see 'time' either) world-lines into place. Probably both. When they get there Carlos cannot see his car, and Juan and Genaro carry on the completely outrageous behavior with large and small objects—rocks, pebbles, roof beams, highly unlikely flies—on the pretext that they are trying to help him find his car. ('Trying' to find something and actually finding it are two entirely dissimilar actions; *not-doings of* one another.) The effort takes on outrageous, exaggerated proportions, until Genaro decides to 'show him the way,' attaches a string to his sombrero and proceeds, successfully, to fly it like a kite."

Coyote: "Now what are the chances of *that*? As Carlos knows full well, this is aerodynamically *impossible* (must be those 'world lines' again) and its actual realization before his very eyes (so much like a movie) forces a 'time superimposed on itself' double-take of the whole deictic situation. In a sudden insight (almost exactly what Don Juan calls *seeing* or 'stopping the world'), Carlos realizes that he will find his lost car in the place where the kite comes down. He does, of course (insight is always a kind of *seeing*) both in spite of and because of the facts that a) *the car was not really there*, and b) *sombreros have few aerodynamic qualifications*."

Roy: "So why didn't the car take off and the sombrero disappear?"

Coyote: "Sometimes I wonder about you professors. Why? For the same reason you get two equipotential solutions to a quadratic equation, Einstein: a positive and a negative—*each the result of false claims made upon the other*, claims that become real once the solution is reached. Why, you Kurt Gödel of the insignificant? Because a negative, or *not-doing*, times another negative, or *not-doing*, always yields a positive result."

Roy: "Thus, to my admittedly dull-witted and altogether professorial mind, Carlos 'finds' an imaginary foreground to his imaginary background and has taken leave, not of his senses but of the *first-attention*, in which, to quote Don Juan, 'all power is trickery.' Now, since everything that Carlos knows or feels about a car—how to recognize it, use it, hide it, find it, drive it—is foregrounded as part of his learned *doing* of things, he is ready to defy the laws of physical reality itself (the defining principle of his *doing*), follow Genaro's example, shift the agentive shift, climb into his not-not real car and, sitting on thin air, drive everybody 'home,' with Don Juan and Don Genaro sitting in the 'back seat,' laughing like children."

Coyote: "So why didn't he just tie a string to his car so he could remember where he left it?"

Roy: "Because, you whipped jackal in wolf's clothing, then the car would have *flown itself* like a kite."

Coyote: "There's something about the *object* that we've been tracking all through these pages—the object as part of the perception that perceives it something about the object and memory, or the juxtaposition of chance and memory, that is not coming through in our explanation. The car is an *object*, right?"

Roy: "In other words, our whole explanation was an attempt to look at Carlos, or car-loss, from the car's point of view, like the Uncertainty Principle is an attempt to look at relativity from the particle's point of view."

Coyote: "An *objective* point of view."

Roy: "As the movie sees the viewer from a differential time frame; it is a matter of *déjà vu* and *vùjá de*."

Coyote: "Come again?"

Roy: "That's the point, isn't it."

Déjà Vu and Vùjá De

Coyote: "Let me get this straight. A *déjà vu* is an uncanny experience, often associated with fatigue, of having had the same experience, or perception, that one is now having, at some time in the past. An experience that one could not otherwise recall without its possible recurrence in that way, as though the workings of memory and chance had somehow gotten confused with one another."

Roy: "An inability on the part of the past to predict the future, or at least its *own* futurity. So what, on that basis, is a *vùjá de*?"

Coyote: "Well, that would be the direct opposite: a *canny* experience, always identified with ebullience, on the part of that experience itself, that *it* had had *you* at some time before."

Roy: "Close, but no cigar. It would be an *in*direct opposite, with the roles of future and past, as well as those of perceiver and perceived, reversed."

Coyote: "Like future-in-its-own-past, and in an *active* rather than a passive mode? Like Carlos's car as *absolutely certain*, it would find him since he was only *relatively certain* he had lost it?"

Roy: "Right. See déjà vu is an *impersonation* of the action of remembering, memory in what a linguist would call an *ergative* modality, a normally active verb or activity expressed in a passive form, with a net gain in the *energy* of the expression itself."

Coyote: "I don't get it."

Roy: "You remember the old Soviet joke: *We pretend to work and the state pretends to pay us.* That would be a double, or *self-reflexive* ergative, like a postmodernist understanding of Marxism or an anthropologist's idea of what the *ritual process* is all about."

Coyote: "So then *vùjá de* would be the total opposite of the ergative mode: an *active* role for the otherwise suborned, or passive subject: not an *impersonation* at all, but an EXPERSONATION. Like saying that 'In this new, liberated Russia *it is the state that pretends to work, whereas the individual, now freed from his worker's chains, has to pay for the whole thing, and REALLY pay.*'"

Roy: "You got it, Coyote; game, set, and match. 'Each being the result of false claims made upon the other.' It's like intention and memory sharing the same basic *description* but having entirely different takes on it. Past its own future and future in its own past are opposite and wholly irreconcilable qualities."

Coyote: "Like you and me: *pest* in his own future and future in his own *pest*."

Roy: "DNA and A.N.D.—'Dat you, Andy?' *Déjà vu* remembers *the intention to remember* but not necessarily the *memory* itself, of which it is quite unsure. *Vùjá de* intends *the memory* but not necessarily the *intention* itself, which it is certain will be recovered, or recollected, at some future time. Hence *déjà vu* is *subjective* and in need of objective corroboration, like Carlos's lost car, whereas *vùjá de* is *objective*, like the car itself, which always was *somewhere* and is in need of subjective retrieval, like Carlos 'finding' it in a place where he never lost it. The default-clause is actually more easily manipulated in prose, which is really past-in-its-own-future, than in immediate experience. For by the time the reader experiences it it is not an immediate experience anymore, but something than happened in the past."

Coyote: "And even more easily manipulated in poetry, like those famous lines of Robert Frost: 'Whose woods dese are I think I know / Ah seed dem someplace else befo.'"

Roy: "Or those less famous lines by Wallace Stevens: 'The trouble with you, Robert, is that you make the visible world too easy to see.'"

Coyote: "And Don Juan makes the *in*visible world impossible to miss."

Roy: "And not because of *word-lines*, either."

Coyote: "Hey Roy, *déjà vu*, didn't I hear you say the same thing before?"

Roy: "Hey Coyote, *vùjá de*, that was our old friend the *Ding an Sich*, the *ungrounded figure of the unfigured ground*, or the *fact without its context and the context without its fact*. Since, as we have learned, the action of 'picturing'—like 'we picture facts to ourselves'—is *reciprocal* between subject and object, so that *facts picture us to themselves* as well."

Coyote: "Say, Roy, why do you *professors*, and especially you *anthropologists*, always talk about something like *pretending* you were explaining it by talking about everything else instead? Like:

I left my double in the day-ja-voo,
doo dah, doo dah,
it looks like me like it looks like you,
oh, *dóò-jà-váy;*
gwanna talk all night,
gwanna talk all day,
de trouble with the double is Don Juan's bubble,
zippity *vóò-jà-dáy.*

The Double
Past in Its Own Future and Future in Its Own Past

Roy: "Fact is, everything in the world we do live in, everything in the world of *fact, time and space, kinship, family, character, personality, love, hate, society, money, objects* is based on *impersonation: world in the person and person in the world*. Like what Aristotle called *mimesis; imitation*—the pretending of similarity in difference and difference in similarity, like *metaphor*. Like Shakespeare: 'All the world's a stage, and we are merely players on it,' like Don Juan's bubble of reflection, you know: 'What you are after is only the *reflection* of your thoughts. You look as you think and you think as you look, and so are trapped in a looking and thinking world.'"

Coyote: "We are fairly consumed by our own self-imitation, aren't we, Roy? By the time any conscious, well-meaning adult reaches maturity, he or she is already living largely in his or her own head. 'Royworld,' as your friend Liz Stassinos called it; 'professor-world' is what I would call it. Remember your *almost perfect* definition of *kinship*?"

Roy: "Sure. 'All we ever know of kinship consists of connections established among the living on behalf of the dead, and connections among the dead established on behalf of the living.'"

Coyote: "A perfect chiasmus, eh? And also what Don Juan calls '*clarity*, the second enemy of the man of knowledge,' the monster hidden in the academic's closet that is *almost a mistake*. A reflection of your own thoughts that has much more to do with *how we think of kinship* than the *actions* that are actually going on out there."

Roy: "I get it—*strategy* is always the *first casualty* on the battlefield, and kinship, like Coyote, is always a *moving target*. Is that what you mean? Like *impersonation* is only the thin edge of the wedge of *expersonation*?"

Coyote: "Yes, Mr. Let's-Talk-About-One-Thing-in-Terms-of-Another, I mean that, and a lot more. I mean the 'moving target' that also *shoots back* at you; for every *déjà vu* there is also a *vùjá de.* I mean that the only thing worth predicting is the unpredictable, and the only thing worth controlling is the uncontrollable. And I mean, most of all, that what you call a 'holographic model' or 'holographic worldview' is one that *imitates you back* with far greater precision and accuracy than you could ever imitate it."

Roy: "So it's like the difference between Karl Pribram's model of the brain and David Bohm's model of the universe. Pribram said that the brain actually functions and thinks *holographically*, effectively realizing the oneness, or mutual occlusion, of part and whole; Bohm called that effect (or also *cause*) the hidden, or *implicate*, structure of the universe itself."

Coyote: "Sure, and as any fool can plainly see, on a part-for-whole basis, the difference between the two is negligible. For as part of the universe, the brain would necessarily incorporate or impersonate the totality of its workings, its *implicate structure*, according to Bohm. Whereas the universe itself would *expersonate* the brain's activity in doing so. You see?"

Roy: "I see, fool that I am, that what the brain impersonates, the universe expersonates, and vice-versa, like *déjà vu* and *vùjá de*: subject and object each re-perceiving the other from its own point of view. I see that this also has something to do with *time*: a past in its own future and a future in its own past. Like there is a huge difference between these two."

Coyote: "Yes, Roy, and you see it in your own particular Royworld kind of way, as you once put it: '*World in the person and person in the world*,' the subject/object flipover, the Gimmick, the rope trick, the disappearing car and the reappearing driver. I'm fine with that. But what you *do not see* is that *both of these things are equal*, and equally *parts* of you and me, and of everybody and everything."

Roy: "And that's what Don Juan calls 'The Double?'"

Coyote: "Among other things, 'There is more in heaven and on earth . . . than is dreamt in your philosophy.'"

Roy: "You mean Shakespeare knew the Double?"

Coyote: "Only in a manner of speaking."

Roy: "Tell me about the Double."

Coyote: "I'll leave that to you. The *recollecting* self, or recollecting part of you, *thinks*, thinks about itself ('remembers' or *imitates* itself) and is incapable of *acting*. IT ONLY *THINKS* IT IS ACTING. The *other* part of you, which we might as well call the *anticipating* self, can ONLY act, and ONLY ACTS AS IF IT WERE THINKING."

Roy: "That means that it actually throws itself blindly into a space it never sees, and does so with perfect accuracy and skill *as if* it were the ultimate acrobat or ballet dancer. As though it knew the steps in advance, in double-time, and as though it acted not only *with* duplicity but *as* duplicity, by remote control, with it, itself, as the *remote*."

Coyote: "Sure, it is not only *gone* by the time you look for it, it's also *gone* by the time *it* looks for it. Which is probably why Don Juan never mentions it, for in fact *it* could never mention itself either. You know the saying, 'What is better than presence of mind in an accident?'"

Roy: "Hell, I even know the answer: absence of body. So in other words *it*, despite the fact that we do not know what *it* is, acts only by accident."

Coyote: "Roy, it *is* accident, the other half of chance that probability has never figured out, being that it can only figure *in*.

Roy: "And which leaves us with *presence of body*, that is, by that time, only a *victim*, a picture of its own pathos."

Coyote: "The recollecting self can only indulge in *fantasies* of moving forward, for it can only *remember* itself doing so."

Roy: "In other words, the recollecting self collects all the *evidence* of action, all your tracks and traces, all the words and noises you leave behind (blah blah blah), and puts them in a big sack, *which is itself*. It is the perfect detective, but *it never solves the crime*."

Coyote: "Why? Since what we call 'thinking' is also *remembering*, it keeps getting behind itself and must *think itself up again* (e.g., what Don Juan calls 'the internal dialogue') every time it thinks. Whereas the anticipatory self is like a joke, always getting ahead of itself, a joke that is always 'on the double,' and *at the expense* of explanation, which can only *redouble its efforts* to tell you about itself."

Roy: "Like *it* . . . went *thataway*, whereas, meanwhile, back at the *ranch* . . . everything was *sacked* because *even 'thataway' went thataway*."

Coyote: "See, Roy, at this juncture in our conversation, which Marshall Sahlins would call 'the structure of the conjuncture,' you are supposed to *ask a question*."

Roy: "Okay, here goes: How can you possibly *know what* he meant by a 'structure of the conjuncture' if neither you nor Marshall can agree on who first came up with the *working misunderstanding*?"

Coyote: "That is not the right question, Roy, it is the *right answer*. The question was supposed to be, 'So why are *they* (the two parts of the Double, or in other words *we*) nearly always convinced that they are one and the same thing?"

Roy: "I get it. Because each one of them, in its own way (the one by thinking as if it were acting, the other by acting as if it were thinking) claims the WHOLE self as itself while having no awareness of the other. Not Being Able To Act The Thinking (as in the case of the recollecting self) and Not Being Able to Think the Acting (as in the case of the anticipating self), are INVISIBLE to one another. And with NO VISIBLE MEANS OF SUPPORT, *anything* is likely to turn tricks."

Coyote: "So it was really Pribram and Bohm all along, or perhaps Shakespeare, and Macbeth: 'Ye canna act the *part*, laddie, wi'oot ya know the *hole*, and ye canna act the *hole*, either, wi'oot ya know the part."

Roy: "So it's *Rob* Roy, is it? It's *about time* [putting on airs]: 'Tomorrow and tomorrow and tomorrow, creeps in this petty pace from day to day, and all our yesterdays have lighted fools the way to dusty death."

Coyote: "So it's past-in-its-own-future and future-in-its-own-past, is it? Like, as I recall, the *Ars Memoria*—a Roman in the gloamin' and a comin' through the wry."

Roy: "To *top it all off*, that so-called invisible body of yours, the *anticipating self*, is what Don Juan calls the *dreaming body*, on the part of the Double that *walks in dreams*, does the impressions of them, makes *other things* visible, and normally keeps itself in the dark."

Coyote: "You mean like the guy who drinks to make *other people* more interesting?"

Roy: "No, I mean like that Chinese dreamer who could not tell whether he was himself dreaming that he was a butterfly, or a butterfly dreaming that it was himself."

Coyote: "Or else, like the Mayan *Hunab Ku*, the 'One and Only God: the One that pictures God as God would picture it and so knows no difference between the two. Knowing for certain that it is a moth in first-attention, because its second-attention, or fly-by-night self, actually *is* a butterfly.'

Roy: "Sure, dreaming bodies don't have to know how to act, they just *act*. And they act *in the future* of their own action, *thataway*."

The Difference between Reality and Itself

Coyote: "Hey, I've just made a brilliant discovery about Don Genaro, Don Juan's immemorial sidekick: he is the very incarnation of all that is right and all that is wrong about our idea of time."

Roy: "You mean like that thing I once said: '*Time is the difference between itself and space; space is the similarity between the two?*'"

Coyote: "Well, you can't be right all of the time, sometimes you've got to be *left*, like for instance *Double or nothing*, two being the operant variable here. Without humor, you see, Genaro would have no power, but without power he would have no humor. So it is between Genaro and his dreaming body, that *the mistrust of humor is a matter of pure mathematics, but the mistrust of mathematics is a matter of pure humor.* They are joined at the hip . . . the REALLY HIP!"

Roy: "Also right, but if both time and humor are the operant variables, as you say—the difference between reality and itself—then the *real* doubling is the essence of Don Juan's teaching. You know, the *balancing act.* So like Genaro's acrobatics between the no-pity, iron discipline that Don Juan calls 'the way of the warrior, or stalker,' and the totally counterintuitive *content* of his knowledge that no one in their right mind would believe without the tricks Genaro plays with it. Like, '*In your dreams,* fella.'"

Coyote: "Like, I mean, *hip to the joint,* or juncture, of the construction. Like *déjà vu* and *vùjá de.* Like the 'enemies of the man of knowledge,' fear, clarity, power, and old age, are what most people would consider as *friends,* or at least 'senior citizens.' Whereas the no nonsense *tough love* pragmatics of Don Juan, so unlike the *empty idealities* that we pretend to live by, are what most people would consider to be enemies."

Roy: "And what has *that* to do with the *contretemps,* as it were, between our two misunderstandings of time: past in its own future and future in its own past?"

Coyote: "For Genaro the difference itself makes all the difference in the world, for he has turned himself (and thus everything else) around in such a way that those two misunderstandings are not misunderstandings at all, but forms of *self-understanding.*"

Roy: " If things didn't work *one* way, they would work *some other* way?"

Coyote: "Nope, always both *ways at once*: not past in its own future but past *as* its own future, and also future *as* its own past."

Roy: "Come again?"

Coyote: "By dint of endless years of iron discipline and careful training, or else pure *dumb luck* (nobody knows for sure, and Genaro isn't telling), Genaro managed to turn his anticipatory self, or dreaming body, into a *perfect simulacrum* of his ordinary physical body, or recollective self. So now he is able to *exercise* (as in 'acrobatics') any of the *limitless possibilities* of the self-anticipating dreaming body within the monochrome spectrum of ordinary physical *doing.* He *is* past *as* its own future by virtue of being also, and at the same time, future *as* its own past."

Roy: "So, let me guess: 'virtue' had absolutely nothing to do with it.

Because Genaro was able to use his anticipating self to *anticipate* his recollective self he was also able to *recollect* his anticipating self, and thus do the thing that the anticipatory self does best of all, which is *disappear*. And is precisely why he isn't around anymore."

Coyote: "Nope, Roy, *wrong again*. See, you get into these little periods of confusion because what Don Juan calls 'the glue that binds our description of time' is still binding you. That was your problem all along, wasn't it? You got *caught in the description*, just like an anthropologist does—you couldn't teach Don Juan because you got caught in the *description* of doing so. But you also couldn't teach the description itself because you got caught in Don Juan. And now you're caught in the description of the Double, and all *doubled up*, and not with laughter, either."

Roy: "So the impersonation of expersonation is *not* the expersonation of impersonation, and the two parts of the double are not *twins* of one another?"

Coyote: "No. To be perfectly correct they are ANTI-TWINS, not only of one another but of everything else as well. But that belongs to *another* description, perfectly correct, that you wrote in another book, called *An Anthropology of the Subject*, a much better book than this one."

Roy: "Does that mean I have to write yet another book?"

Coyote: "No, that would mean getting caught in *another* description, wouldn't it? It means you have to get *this one* straight, for once and for all. For NOW is the only time there ever was, or is, or could be."

Roy: "And *that* would mean that I have become *unstuck*, or *unglued*, as per Don Juan's description, of the glue that binds our description of time. And that, *in turn*, would mean that NOW, being only a *descriptive* term, is NOT the only time there ever was, or is, or could be, because by the time you even think of it as a *now* it is already a THEN. And on *prima facie* evidence, or description (take your pick) *then* is the only kind of time there ever was, or is, or could be."

Coyote (examining Roy for traces of *sanity*): "Boy, you sure *have* become unstuck, this time with crazy glue, for NOW you have not only gotten caught in a *description* but in *the description of description*, like a phenomenologist. I believe it was Kurt Gödel who pointed out, to Albert Einstein no less, that what he thought of as time—the 'fourth dimension'—was really only *space*, like 'the space of time,' and that what is *past* is already *gone* by the time you try to remember it."

Roy (examining Coyote for traces of *in*sanity): "Now *that*, if you will recall, is exactly the description, in no uncertain terms, of the *anticipating self*, also *gone by the time you try to remember it*. And it *stands to reason* (whereas you can only sit and scratch) that, as I have already written, in what you called a 'better book than this one,' *space is the only kind of time that is still around, and that really matters*—all at *once*, as a matter of fact. And, furthermore, though I may be after the *description of a description*, like any flea-bitten phenomenologist, but you yourself are after the *description of the description of a nondescription*, you nondescript cur."

Coyote (making as if to scratch for nonexistent fleas): "Now this is getting us *nowhere*, Roy, and as for *description*, the only real description of time is the time of the description, or, in other words, its Double."

Roy: " That would mean that the anticipatory self, or *natural*, as Don Juan calls it, is itself what we have called 'time.'"

Coyote: "It's own not-doing, and the difference between itself and space."

Roy: "Now we are getting down to brass tacks, or at least to *ass-tracks*."

The Nagual

Coyote: "*Nagual* has no *limitations at all*, and is defined that way, which of course means that no one could ever know it or control it by virtue of the fact that it could never know or control itself. There is no such thing as a *part* of the nagual, nor, for the same reason, the *whole* of the nagual. Holography, in other words, is just a way of *describing* it, which it can only do by describing itself."

Roy: "So how would one 'get to' the nagual, as Don Juan and Don Genaro seem to be able to do?"

Coyote: "One doesn't get to *it*; *it* gets to one instead. One does not cause it—*it affects* one."

Roy: "Then how would one 'affect' the nagual, if the person, or human impersonation, has no purchase over it?"

Coyote: "By an act of total *expersonation*, acting with what Don Juan calls *pure abandon*. Like you're falling from a plane at 6,000 feet, with *no visible means of support*—no parachute to cushion your fall. And you say to yourself, "Looks like I have only a few seconds to live; *might as well enjoy it*.""

Roy: "That actually happened, to a real person?"

Coyote: "It happened to *the most real person you ever knew*!"

Roy: "Like the nagual *makes love to you*?"

Coyote: "And *then some*, but you don't want to know about *them*."

Roy: "But I do want to know about *her*."

Coyote: "What did she say about it?"

Roy: "Well, for years she couldn't remember what exactly had taken place, but later she said, 'I remember just a little bit—two *beings* helped me down.'"

Coyote: "And we know exactly who those two beings were, don't we?"

Roy: "We sure as hell *do not*."

Coyote: " What did she say about them?"

Roy: "Well, nothing, really. Except later, on another occasion, when talking about some other people, she said, 'They had each defined themselves as superior to one another, *and that makes a bond stronger than love*.'"

Coyote: "For most of us, however, the position of the nagual is the exact opposite of this; it has an *inferiority complex*. It is *repressed*. You would be, too, if you spent most of your life locked in a cellar, treated like a crazy person."

Roy: "I would want to *kick ass*; I would want to *kill everybody*!"

Coyote: "Right."

The Tonal

Roy: "So the nagual has no real existence, or nonexistence either, and can only 'act' in the way that the anticipatory self acts: *by taking leave of itself.* Not pursuing, but actually being pursued by the illusion that it might have a real existence."

Coyote: "In other words, it cannot know, but can only *know from itself,* and cannot act, in any real sense, unless it *acts out.*"

Roy: "And it could not act out unless it was already acting *in,* that is, in the guise of something else, which we call the *tonal* and which represses the hell out of it for the sake of its own sweet self-importance."

Coyote: "So let me get this straight: the nagual could not *possibly* exist without the tonal."

Roy: "Nor *impossibly*—which is usually the case—either. They have each defined, or undefined, themselves as being in some way superior to the other, and that makes a bond stronger than . . . "

Coyote: "NOT love. Hell, stronger than EXISTENCE would be more like it."

Roy: "So all those philosophers who have talked about the equivalence of holography and love . . . "

Coyote: "Might just as well be talking about the tonal, or else they have not dropped 6,000 feet without a chute and *survived.*"

Roy: "Most of them are dead, in any case."

Coyote: "Good."

Roy: "Why do you get nasty like that?"

Coyote: "Because *you* had a fling with the most real person in the world, and I did not."

Roy: "Aha. Jealous."

Coyote: "The only reason the tonal and the nagual can exist is because of mutual jealousy."

Roy: [begins to whistle *Carmen*] "So why did you call her the most real person in the world?"

Coyote: "Because I am beginning to have my doubts about that, and the best way to get the better of my doubt is to be jealous of it."

Roy: "The most useful definition of tonal would be an *assemblage*, like the sack of evidences that the recollecting self collects, all the tracks and traces, you know; the 'hunting and gathering' lifestyle that might be confused with *culture*."

Coyote: "So a modern anthropologist would say that people do not *eat* anymore, they do something else called FOODING. And they do not really *mate*, the way animals are said to do, but do something else called CLONING. In other words they are not doing anything USEFUL anymore, but something rather more argumentative, like what the postmodernists would call POLITICAL."

Roy: "Like a wolf in sheep's clothing, eh? So what are they *really* doing?"

Coyote: "What they are really doing is a *third* thing, which you have called *obviation*. Which turns out to be the most *effective* definition of tonal: staging a sort of internal competition with itself or with the world—take your pick—a self-descriptive *reductionism* of pairing words or concepts with one another, as Don Juan puts it, in order to name its *opposite*. 'Name it and nail it,' as the saying goes."

Roy: "And so cultures keep turning into other cultures, languages into other languages, concepts into other concepts, religions into other religions, all in a studied and desperate attempt to discover what it is that makes them want to do such a thing."

Coyote: [singing under his breath "Leprosy, she gave me lepro-sy"] Like the geneticist who is looking for the gene that makes people want to discover genes. And so the process will never complete itself because the secret of what it is looking for is the very process by which it is looking."

Roy: "In other words, the key word in everything we have just been talking about—MATING, CLONING, OBVIATION—is *pairing*, making *pairs* of things in order to eliminate, and finding out which of the pair is the more meaningful so you can get on to the next pair. And the next, and the next—you could make a sort of tree-diagram, or chain of triangles."

Coyote: "We shall get to that in another chapter; all we have got to do now, for the time being, is . . . "

Roy: "I dare you to complete that sentence."

Coyote: "There is no definition of the tonal."

Roy: "*Wrong.* There are *too many* definitions of tonal, and we do ourselves the disservice of calling them cultures, trying to live with them, imagining that, in some way, they may be able to *solve* each other, like puzzles."

Coyote: "The simple word, or concept, *tonal.* 'All the words you know, and all the things (for example, combinations, syntaxes) that those words mean, or *by which they possibly could mean,'* may be substituted for any subject, any discipline or methodology, or science, or art, or philosophy that the mind can conceive, and so *consummate* our thinking on that subject. In that sense tonal is *the discipline of all disciplines,* 'world in the person and person in the world.'

Roy: "Would that mean that *substitution* itself, or *the substitution of substitution for anything else,* is tonal? Like the description of description itself that gets lost in its own description?"

Coyote: "Not at all. When you talk that way you are beginning to talk about something else instead: the *obviation* or self-revealing auto-reductive process that is, so to speak, the thin edge of the wedge of nagual."

Roy: "Like, 'She fills a much-needed gap in the hitherto self-assured, totally logical and completely self-understandable structure of our *affair,* or tonal—take your pick.'"

Coyote: "*Leave her alone,* Roy. She has already recovered from her fall through the sky. 'Dances With Gravity,' I believe you called her. Whereas *you,* it appears, *have not.*"

Roy: "Define obviation."

Coyote: "That's the *point,* isn't it? Like you never got that 'pairing' thing down Pat, or whatever her name was. The term 'obviation' comes from the Latin *ob via,* literally 'in the way.' The dictionary definition of *obviate* is 'to anticipate and dispose of.'"

Roy: "So that would be tonal's version of the nagual, like the *antici-*

patory self we were talking about, in the *recollective* self's version of it, or what Don Juan called 'the somersault of thought into the impossible' or 'the ulterior configuration of the abstract.' It's what Goethe called the exact, concrete imagination.

Coyote: "There were some pretty formidable traditions behind the teachings of Don Juan, weren't there? Like the Meso-Americans with their 'Lord of the Center and the Periphery' and their 'One and Only God,' or the Aztec *Moyucoyani*, 'The God that Invented Itself.'

Roy: "AWESOME would be the word for it, like the *Faustian*, Spengler's favorite, named after the guy who sold his soul to the devil in return for power and *is still doing it*."

Coyote: "So you see what those Meso-American people were after with their extravagant and intensely horrific god-images, like 'The Flayed God, or the 'Lord of the Smoking Mirror,' or the polysynthetic, often *synesthetic* (as in 'synesthesia'—crosscutting and appealing to all the senses at once) pan-illusional technologies of their architecture?"

Roy: "Obviation?"

Coyote: "No, obviation with a VENGEANCE, like Lyndon Johnson's 'Grab 'em by the balls and their hearts and minds will follow.' Like DRAMA. Like, 'don't just *convince* them, BLOW THEIR MINDS!"

Roy: "Like the slogan I once saw on the frieze of a thirteenth-century ballroom in the south of England, which the archae-ologists had just revealed under centuries of over-plastering. It said: DREDE GODDE, '*dread* God,' like 'Hey, buddy, I don't care what you believe or disbelieve about *anything*: RUN. LIKE. HELL.'"

Coyote: "Just like disappearing cars, eh?"

Roy: "More like disappearing WHOLE WORLDS!"

Coyote: "As Dorothy would say, we're not exactly in Kansas anymore."

Roy: "And certainly not in the tonal nor, come to think of it, the nagual either."

Recapitulation

Coyote: "That's the point, isn't it? Schneider's Law all over again: 'If things did not work *this* way, they would work *some other way*.'"

Roy: "Why not simply, 'If things did not *break down* one way, they would break down some other way?' Kind of cracks you up, doesn't it?"

Coyote: "*Won't work*; that would be the downsized, insidiously privatized, or in other words (and what is the tonal but *other words*) *computerized* version of Murphy's Law. Roy, let me tell you a thing or two about *originality*."

Roy: "What is it you wanted to tell me about originality?"

Coyote: "I forget."

Roy: "In that case it must be a working misunderstanding."

Coyote: "A working misunderstanding about what?"

Roy: "A working misunderstanding about who *originally* came up with the idea of a working misunderstanding, or, *in other words*, what the hell do you think Marshall Sahlins, Jim Bohannan, and I have being *doing* all of these years?"

Coyote: "Mercury's Law."

Roy: "*Mercury's* Law? What the hell is that?"

Coyote: "Absolutely nothing. Or, in other words, I forget. Or maybe I didn't forget and someone stole my message."

Roy: "*Which* message?"

Coyote: "Why, my *original* one. See, Mercury was the ancient Roman god of limits and boundaries, hermetically sealed, as it were, and famous for his double-duty act of poisoning swordfish and stealing messages, at the same time."

Roy: "I see, it's a *defunct foil*, like 'better a dead swordfish than a live herm-e-NEWT.'"

Coyote: "Sure. See, a *live* hermeneut would be *a contradistinction in terms*."

Roy: "So what is Mercury's Law?"

Coyote: "An insidious sub-version of Wagner's Law: 'Of all the things that could possibly happen in the next moment, *absolutely none of them will*.' Because, you see, all of them have already happened before, and even before that, which, my friend, is the full and complete definition of the tonal and the *only word you know* that absolutely forbids the possibility of an afterward."

Roy: "Except, of course, in *recapitulation.*"

Coyote: "Of all the cheap gin-joints in the world. . . . So it really comes down to *pairing*, or duality, like that of tonal and nagual, which are each so much *about themselves* that their self-invisible codependency, *by definition*, upon one another, is the only real thing about them. Like, you are never going to find an example of tonal all by itself without its inherent tendency to name its opposite. And you are never going to find an example of nagual all by itself but that it will be the *next* thing that will happen after the one you were expecting. And so on."

Roy: "So why bother to make the distinction at all?"

Coyote: "So that the distinction, as it were, does not *make us*, from the *inside* instead of the outside. Like that Daribi truism about our so-called reproduction, that '*a child is a wound from within.*' Or like that *most real person in the world*, whom you never got over, who turned you into the most *unreal* person in the world."

Roy: "And made you the most unreal coyote in the cosmos."

Coyote: "Then what Castaneda calls 'recapitulation' is not just another mind-numbing New Age exercise in oversimplification, another impersonation of people, or, as you call them, *cultures*, impersonating one another."

Roy: "Tell me about it."

Coyote: "Well, the problem with the *twins*, or mutual impersonations of one another, is that they are really *anti-twins*, mutual EX-PERSONATIONS of one another, joined at the hip and *looking for love.*"

Roy: "Actually it is *too funny* to tell me about; you'd better *show me.*"

Coyote: "Then it's the pairing of pairing itself with *unpairing*, or a*symmetry*. What Don Juan calls a not-doing, or how the recollecting self and the anticipating self have nothing to do with one another. That's the funny edge, see?"

Roy: "No, I *don't see.*"

Coyote: "It is as though two anthropologists, looking for the secret of the *incest taboo*, stumbled upon its indirect opposite, the OUTCEST TABOO."

Roy: "Incest, or the taboo on incest, is the most quizzical thing the human race has ever had to face."

Coyote: "Sure, and it is largely *honored in the breach*, if not the *breech*. It's like that old German song about 'The one of them is stolen and the other isn't theirs.'"

Roy: "Let me get this straight (as Adam said to Eve): *Gender* twins us *outward* into two distinctive body types, which we call 'male' and 'female,' whereas *laterality*—the 'sidedness' or right-left dimension of the world) or the brain-body complex (take your pick, we always do)—twins each and every one of us *inward* into a *single individual organism*, or at least *orgasm*. Where do you get this stuff about 'the one of them is stolen and the other isn't theirs?'"

Coyote: "Well, you had to be *told* which gender you were, and what gender is, didn't you? What it is and how it *operates*, like you didn't know it by *instinct*. And then, when you did learn, you could only do so by referring it to the other form of twinning—*laterality*—because that is the only way we can make *distinctions*."

Roy: (quoting Brer Rabbit) "*Born and bred in de briar patch*. But it all fell apart when I met *her*, the most real person in the world. And why is dat, Brer Coyote, why is dat?"

Coyote: "Because, my tarred-and-feathered friend, you had become *unstuck*. Because, anthropologist that you were, you had lost any semblance of *objectivity*. But mainly because, and mostly because, *gender, taken in and of itself, is a purely subjective direction*, just as *laterality, taken in and of itself, is a purely subjective direction*. Look in a mirror sometime, son—depends on which way you are facing."

Roy: "Like I was using one subjective set of directions to tell me about the other, and then the *other* set of subjective directions to tell me about the *one*. I can tell them together, but how do I tell them apart?"

Coyote: "Like they say in Harlem, 'You can dream it *up*, but can you dream it *down*?' You were the creature of your own *impersonations*, tonal/tonal comparisons, face-to-face relationships—kinsmen, mothers, sweethearts, what you called, as I recall, 'Burgundy Adultery.' And what you really needed was *two beings to help you down*."

Roy: "In other words, the ANTI-TWINS, EXPERSONATION, THE OUTCEST TABOO. Tell me about them, Coyote!"

Coyote: "DREDE GODDE, Roy, I'll have to *show* you. See, humanity would never be humanity, get over its dang-blasted *impersonations* of itself, if it did not have a *foil—an ulterior configuration of its abstractness*. I'd show you what this means but then I'd have to *kill* you."

Roy: "I'll take your *recapitulation* as a show of good faith."

Coyote: "And instantly regret it, because *one of them is stolen and the other isn't theirs*. Like we have to steal from laterality to know the one-sidedness of our own-gendered being—the Mobius strip-tease of the fact that *every person on this earth belongs to a single gender, called 'own gender,' which is the one gender they happen to own up to*."

Roy: "And that means that *no one on this earth belongs to the other gender*, because that is the one that no one happens to own."

Coyote: "Sure, 'the other isn't theirs.' Though in the case where that other gender happens to be female, *she* owns *you* instead. Why, she could even be your mother. Thus if the *lateral* version of own gender is shaped like a Mobius, the *lineal* version is shaped like a Klein-bottle. You know, first she *impersonates* you, *litterally*, on the inside, and then she *expersonates* you, *figuratively*, on the outside, but she's always your mother, both ways at once."

Roy: "Like we have to steal from gender to know the inside from the outside, or, *figuratively* speaking, the mother from the self. So where does the incest taboo fit in?"

Coyote: "Well, see, that's the point: you don't want to be *outside* of your mother and *inside* of your mother both at the same time. One of them is stolen and the other isn't yours."

Roy: "Look, Mr. Smarty-pants, as an *anthropologist* I happen to know that maternal incest is only one of a great many forms of incest, which is understood very differently in the many different cultures."

Coyote: "But you don't know the *Tao* very well, do you. And the *Tao* happens to be the *Way*, and the way begins with the statement that '*The named is the mother of the myriad creatures*.'"

Roy: "So, in other words, every time I call somebody *names* I am committing incest?"

Coyote: "No, that's just the *primordial* incest, like talking about one thing by talking about everything else instead. *Professor*. To get to the real *point* of this discussion, which is OUTCEST, we shall have to *recapitulate*."

Roy: "Not *again*."

Coyote: "It's the only *Way*."

Roy: "Sigh!"

Coyote: "*Humanity*, as well as a great many other creatures, is constituted in only one way, which we have distinguished as *twinning* and which consists in twinning a single thing *outward*, in the form of two distinctive body types, called *genders*, and then twinning *that very same thing inward* to form the distinctive (and distinguishing) *laterality* of the *single individual*."

Roy: "Well, that sure does sound to me like a recapitulation: the one of them is stolen and the other—why *it's not even the other* because, and *mark my words*, the *objectivity* of each form of twinning is based entirely on the *subjectivity* of the other. There is *no end in sight*."

Coyote: "So it went on for billions of years: the myriad creatures interbreeding promiscuously with one another, committing unspeakable acts of *interspecific incest*, which you, in your case, call 'evolution.' Then one day, from out of the blue. . ."

Roy: "Don't hold your breath; it's healthier to *give it up* . . ."

Coyote: ". . . came the ANTI-TWINS, the GENDER SYMME-TRIES, the (expletive deleted) EXPERSONIFIERS, the ANTI-TONAL ANTI-NAGUALS."

Roy: "And what difference did they make?"

Coyote: "All the difference in the world. And so, in fact, the world;

they are the Ones by which we know from ourselves—and also subjectivity from objectivity—and we know these things by knowing the one from the other."

Roy: "So what are their names?"

Coyote: "The One is called *The Two of One* or *The Icon of Incest*, like the *bad example*, getting caught in the description. The Other is called *The One of Two* or *The Adult Embryo*, like the *good example, not* getting caught in the description."

Roy: "How can something with no description catch anything at all, and how can something so full of its own description get caught?"

Coyote: "Ask yourself, Roy: how did *we* survive this chapter?"

Roy: "We didn't."

Coyote: "Now you're beginning to catch on. *We* are constituted by gender twinned *outward*, whereas they are constituted by gender twinned *inward*. It's the most general definition of incest imaginable. And we are constituted by laterality twinned *inward*, concentrated on the inner core of the body, whereas they are constituted by laterality twinned outward, which is the most general definition of technology imaginable. They are like the tool using *us*, and they are like *incest* using us."

Roy: "Holy smoke, Coyote, do you know what that *means*? It means that they have *obviated* the difference between subjectivity and objectivity—like those so-called UFO aliens—so that *even they* could not tell where they came from or where they were going. They are *neotones*, totally neotenous *beings*, mere fakes of the fakes we have always suspected them to be. *And it gets worse*, because if you put all of this stuff together it turns out that it falls apart because they are constructed in a completely *apposite* way to the way we are: *they are bi-gendered beings with only one side each*."

Coyote: "Holy mushroom cloud, Roy, that means we have been *replaced*, and not by computers either. Replaced by beings who are not only more one-sided than we are but also *much more real*. So real, in fact, that they are practically invisible to us, and we must *infer* them, in the way that a blind person is obliged to infer humor."

Roy: "Do you supposed Don Juan knew about them, like the ones he called the *allies*, or inorganic awarenesses?"

Coyote: "Not a chance. Because if *he* knew about them, he being a Nagual and all, he could never *burn with the fire from within* and exit this world in triumph with his warriors' party streaming behind him."

Roy: "Where did we go wrong, Coyote, that we are not *warriors* like *him*?"

Coyote: "Must be our *vocation*, since that seems to be the only part of us that is still around."

Roy: "Well, I guess. When I was young, I wanted to be an astronomer."

Coyote: ""Why, to avoid the draft?"

Roy: "Not getting caught in the *conscription*? Hey, that's good. But it was really a sort of *moonlighting*:

The work of war is *fighting over fight*,
the business-end of business: *rob 'em blind*,
Proctology is never far behind,
the work of gods: *preposterating might*!
A shrewd accountant's work is *countersigned*
to re-indemnify the word "indict,"
the job of stars is *staying up all night*
to intimate insouciance to the mind."

Coyote: "A matter of *vocation*, as it were;
when day is done, *pretending to evolve*
is such a bloody bore that giving lip
disservice to the moon's the only cure,
no hassle, no more problems left to solve,
so quit your day-job, *night* is such a trip!"

2 | EXPERSONATION

The Coyote of Anthropology

Roy: "This is a coyote tale told to Frank Hamilton Cushing by the Zuni people."
Coyote: "And, of course, thoroughly *spoiled* by You-Know-Who."

Two RAVENS were *racing their eyes*. They were sitting on a bluff, detaching their eyes from their sockets (craack—POP) and sending them flying around the landscape. FOR FUN. Feeling the distances and perimeters of things. Then they would fly them back and secure them (POP—craack) back into their sockets.

COYOTE had never seen such a sight before; he was curious, he was delighted, and he was yellow. He trotted over to the RAVENS and said "teach me that trick; teach me how to race my eyes."

"Oho," said the RAVENS, and "Aha," said the RAVENS. "Eyes bigger than your stomach, hey?"

"You don't know the half of it."

"Well, my legs get sort of tired, trotting around like this, and would I could fly my sight around the whole friggin' landscape, and but stay in one place, like you."

"Well, in that case," said the corvine competitors, those that Two Crows could not deny, "do it like this: (craack—POP) see? And (craack—POP) see?"

"Done and done," said COYOTE, and his eyes took off, flying all around the place, sniffing all the rocks and crevices, DAWG NABBIT you know. COYOTE waited and waited, anxious for a little insight, but in point of fact the eyes never came back.

"Aha," said the RAVENS, and "Oho," said the RAVENS. "We'll help you find them." (In RAVEN talk this means "Nevermore.") Find them they did, goggling about, and in point of fact they ATE them, then went on their merry way.

After a while COYOTE began to get the gist of it, or at least the *punch-line* (like: SOCKET TO ME!), and he started, feeling blindly, to recover his missing orbs. He groped and he groped ("Aha" and "Oho"), and when he found some squish things under a bush he screwed them (squish—squish—PLOP) back into his sockets. But they were only scrawny little yellow berries, and since then COYOTE has only looked with a squint, with very weak, yellow eyes.

Roy: "The eye, they say, is not part of the body."

Coyote: "What is this, *folklore*?"

Roy: "No, folklore is the kind of thing folks pretend *not* to believe in, so it must be true. In a certain highly important sense one may say that the *body*—or what is called *embodiment*—is really part of the eye, since all the significant details whereby the visual is confused with *reality* are actually re-projected within the eye."

Coyote: "So then the eye and its *field of vision* are parts of the same *figure-ground reversal*, given that the eye cannot see itself and is never within its own *field of vision* (though that field of vision is always within the eye). Same perspective; different perspex."

Roy: "Yup, in anthropology they call this 'perspectivism,' but in perspective they call it 'anthropology.' What the one impersonates the other expersonates, and vice-versa. See, the eye is like the objective lens of a telescope or movie projector, in which the whole encompassing *image*—of *anything*—is twisted around and inverted on itself, actually reduced to an *infinitesimal point*, before it can be spread out again into a meaningful picture."

Coyote: "*Lak mamaran*, literally 'luck in the double-focus,' is how the Barok people of New Ireland put this when they want to wish someone well. It is like the *Aleph* that Jorge Luis Borges writes about, the possibility that, since all meaningful details must be contracted to an infinitesimal point in the act of perception, *all of them actually are*, and that single point exists somewhere on this earth."

Roy: "Whereas we know for a fact that it exists *everywhere*, in every possible contingency, given that the eye belongs to the body quite as much as the body belongs to the eye. So it may be that we are talking about the *soul*—that otherwise mysterious quality—instead of the simple thing we call *vision*."

Coyote: "And that would mean that the actual *physical* body itself is part of that vision, tactility and all—all the senses in a single focus. Like that amazing example of *physiognomic tact* that Jeffrey Clark reported for the Wiru people of Papua New Guinea, the neighbors of the Daribi. According to Jeffrey, the Wiru call the *physical* body the *picture soul* of a person, the *impersonation of its expersonation*. Or is it the other way around?"

Roy: "Well, for the Daribi themselves it *is* the other way around; not the *picture-soul* but the *soul-picture*. What Don Juan calls the *luminous body*, the Hindus call *the subtle body*, and the Chinese call the *chi*. Daribi call it the *bidinoma*,' and it actually happened to me."

Coyote: "*Happening* is a very funny way to put your *whole existence*."

Roy: "One evening in 2000 I was walking across the Karimui airstrip—the only really cleared area in the region—with some young Daribi kids. The kids were dumbfounded by their long shadows projected across the field by the setting sun. 'Wow,' they said, 'SOULS!' and then they giggled."

Coyote: "That, too, is a funny way to put your whole existence."

Roy: "Next day I took the matter up with my friend Danu, the magistrate: 'Why is it that you people identify the animating principle, that thing you call the *bidinoma*, with the shadow, or name, or photograph of a person?'"

Coyote: "And he gave you the Daribi blessing, didn't he: *po mene*, 'no talk,' an expression of extreme satisfaction or annoyance."

Roy: "As a matter of fact he *did not*. He simply said 'I'll show you. Stand over there, Roy, and stare at your black shadow on the ground. When you are finished, look up at the blue sky and tell me what you see.' I did as I was told, and when I looked up at the sky I saw a visual effect, a rods-and-cones afterimage of the dark silhouette I had just been staring at—a glowing, luminous *shape* of my body floating in the blue."

Coyote: "And you said something like 'That's *it?*' or 'That's *all?*'"

Roy: "*Something* like that. And he said, 'Well, it ANIMATED you, didn't it?'"

Coyote: "So was it your *impersonation* looking at your *expersonation*, or your *expersonation* looking at your *impersonation?*"

Roy: "That's IT, Coyote, you *got it in one*. Next time try flipping a coin with only one side. That very same point of befuddlement—'a mere shadow of my former self' or 'why do you folks equate the shadow with the soul,' has a long, pompous, and very quizzical history in the annals of human self-examination."

Coyote: "Don't tell me, let me guess: 'The first time as tragedy, the second time as pure farce.'"

Roy: "It's even worse. Back in the days of Sir James Frazer, it was elevated to the status of a universal 'primitive' religion called ANIMISM."

Coyote: "Whereas it was really luck in the double focus. DUMB luck."

Roy: "Sure was, because much later, after Frazer and even Freud had had their tilt with it, it became the focal point of another, and this time *truly* primitive, pseudo-religion. *This* time it was called New Age Spirituality, the enlightened rediscovery of the *chi*, the *aura*, the subtle body, and the luminous egg."

Coyote: "So the whole tragicomedy of the *flipover* in human self-examination, from the *supernatural* to the *natural* to the New Age, had nothing to do with the evolution of science?"

Roy: "Quite the contrary, it had *everything* to do with the evolution of science."

Coyote: "You know what *that* means, don't you? It means that the Lore Folk, on a *strictly empirical basis*, are the *expersonative reciprocals* of folklore."

The Lore Folk

Roy: "You mean like subject/object shift, like *dèjá vu* and *vùjá de*? Just who, exactly, are the Lore Folk?"

Coyote: "You name it: ghosts, poltergeists, the *unexplained*; *the Little Folk*, the place-spirit, imps, demons, incubae and succubae, objects and subjects that behave strangely, probably angels and miracles, and any of the countless so-called *imaginaries* that people all over the world have been experiencing as real for tens of thousands of years. And that means, especially, *cats*."

Roy: "But that must mean that just as *we*, on our part, pretend *not* to believe in them, so *they*, for their part, likewise pretend not to believe in *us*."

Coyote: "On a *strictly empirical basis*, like Carlos's disappearing car, which we already 'examined.' Believe me, they are *not* supernatural, and neither are they accidentally or deliberately contrived 'special effects' generated by coincidence out of purely natural phenomena. They are totally *scientific*, having nothing to do with either belief or disbelief."

Roy: "They are scientific, then, in the only way that anthropology can be scientific, or science itself can be anthropological: by gauging the difference between background assumptions and foreground projections."

Coyote: "But that would mean that the Anti-twins, or Don Juan's conception of the Double, are not simply *models*, or *images*, or *concepts*, in the way that scientists have understood these things. It would mean that, like the Mobius Strip or the Klein bottle, they are subject/object shift *agencies*, that either turn *us* inside-out or show *us* to be one-sided."

Roy: "And that, *in turn*, would mean, following our previous discussion, , that *gender*—both one-sided and two-sides-at-once—is also one of the Lore-Folk, or at least two—remember, *other gender* is a creature that no one has ever *been* or *met*."

Coyote: "And it would also mean, via the Anti-twins, that *laterality* is as well, and thus the *difference* between gender and laterality, and thus, also, *any* difference. Including not only your dratted love life—'how we all get lost in our descriptions'—but also *vocation*. Remember our *sonnet?*"

Roy: "Nope, I must have gotten lost in my own description."

Coyote: "Well, then, that is exactly what *vocation* means. A *sonnet*, carefully understood and constructed *on a strictly empirical basis* is a perfect example of a description getting lost in its own description."

Roy: "No, Coyote, *on a strictly empirical basis*, as you say, and speaking of the Lore Folk, as we were, a sonnet is a *weapon*:

Weapons

The earliest we find were shaped in stone
by almost-random blows, yet clearly planned—
as easy, to make, then, as understand,
and each successive epoch mind has known
has trafficked in this deadly contraband,
as if men's dreams had nightmares of their
own; with every age of reason they have grown
more accurate, more balanced in the hand.

The Will is beautiful when cast in steel,
honed clean and rubbed until it holds the
glance in sudden portraiture, amazed, betrayed,
as many a warrior, stunned and brought to
heel has ridden deathward, hurled on by his
lance, drawn by his pistol, burnished by his blade.

Coyote: "So, Roy, *word-games make us proud to die*, hey? Expersonation is not a vocation but a weapon, hey? You and your 'sudden portraiture,' your dratted love-life—you were never very good at *romance*, were you?"

Roy: "No, I left that to the crying-towel phenomenologists."

Coyote:"Well I'll show you classical, and I'll show you *class*, and I'll show you *expersonation*, up your _____ "

Roy: "Up yours, too. No need to get die-a-critical about it; you were meaning to show me that, in strictly empirical terms, other gender, the bizarre creature than no one has ever met, or known, is the most deadly weapon of all, far more deadly than the sonnet."

Coyote: "*Show* you, hell, I mean to *tell* you, in your own words:

Snowfall

My love has got to be so way away
that each snow drops its shadow in between;
where death and twilight were not meant to
mean there are no bridges to her snowy day,
no rivers vocable, no roads come clean,
no truths to launder, syllables to say,
no chess of attitude, no piece to play
to white's advantage; isolate her queen.

Ice crystals have a crisp and furry tongue;
the wind gives grounds for tonsillectomy.
Her hips broke low, made up for that in
savvy, *gluteus maximus*, but none too heavy—
but I digress, how incorrect of me;
THE LION AND THE HE-BEAR EAT THEIR YOUNG."

Roy: "That old *wound from within*, hey? So now it's *protest masculinity*, hey?"

Coyote: "What other kind of masculinity *is* there?"

Roy: "*Expersonation*, that's what. It's my whole vocation."

Coyote: "So why are you not an astronomer, like a *real star*?"

Roy: "Well, I always wanted to be an astronomer in high school. But then I made a mistake on my SAT exam, a real glitch; I got as high a score on my math achievement test as on my verbal."

Coyote: "Tsk tsk, Dumb Luck. Your verbal score was probably ruined by writing *sonnets*."

Roy: "And before I could apologize they sent a nice professor from CalTech to interview me for admission."

Coyote: "And you apologized to him?"

Roy: "Hell no; I had never gotten a grade higher than C-minus in any of my math courses. I simply lectured him, nonstop, on the structure and the function of the sonnet."

Coyote: "So why didn't you read him one of your sonnets?"

Roy: "ARE YOU KIDDING? He was an *English* professor."

Coyote: "Like you said, a sonnet is a *weapon*."

Roy: "And I had not even met up with *other gender* yet.

Coyote: "No one ever has—other gender is a very lonely thing. So where are you in your life now, Roy?"

Roy: "Absolutely *nowhere*."

Coyote: "Whereas an *astronomer*, of course, would be *relatively* everywhere. So how did *you* get to be absolutely nowhere?"

Roy: "It's a long story."

Coyote: "How does it begin?"

Roy: "*Expersonation*: 'Two RAVENS were racing their eyes.'"

Expersonation as Vocation

Coyote: "So it really began when you were a graduate student at the University of Chicago."

Roy: "The sun was already up on the morning of May 25, 1963, as I lay in my bed at International House, dreaming. I had expected to do field research among the Australian aborigines, and in my dream I had boarded an airliner and was on my way to Australia. In midflight, however, the airliner turned suddenly into a single-engine Cessna; I was sitting next to the pilot, and we were making a landing approach to a grass airstrip bordered by banana trees, with blue mountains in the distance. MY GOD—the dream snapped into lucidity—THIS IS NEW GUINEA, and it was either that, or a loud buzzing sound, that brought me into full awareness. They were buzzing my room to announce the arrival of a telegram from the University of Washington, informing me of my field grant."

Coyote: "The Fates lead the willing, the unwilling they *drag*."

Roy: "Out of BED?"

Coyote: "Out of *sight*, Roy."

Roy: "It goes on, Coyote, it *gets worse*. Four months later I found myself sitting next to the pilot of a Territory Airlines Cessna, flying over the razorback ridges of highland New Guinea. 'See that broken one on the horizon?' the pilot said. 'That is Mt. Karimui.' The plane circled downward and swung over a flat forested plateau and began its landing approach to the by now familiar grass strip bordered by banana trees with blue mountains in the distance."

Coyote: "There is no such thing as a lapse, or duration, of time. Time only *pretends* to pass so that we may see ourselves in it. It is like a parallax, or stereoscopic view of things: past remembering the future so that future may remember the past."

Roy: "And then he got NASTY. *Segue*: June 2000. The sun is already up. I awaken in my tent in Kurube Village, get out of my sleeping bag, and step outside. There on a branch over my tent is a sharp-looking black bird, flirting acrobatically as though to call attention to itself. It was my first sight of the *kauweri*, the Black Butcher Bird, the messenger that, according to Daribi mythology, had caused humankind to lose its gift of immortality."

Coyote: "There is no such thing as immortality, or mortality, either—*each being the result of false claims made upon the other.* There is only the mountain, Karimui—'Migaru' or 'Korobo'—an immense, self-destructive disaster waiting to happen that has never looked the same way twice. Which has blown up many many times, strewing house-sized boulders across the plateau, incinerating all inhabitants in the very air they stood in with its pyroclastic cloud."

Roy: "A once-in-a-lifetime bird-watching experience! I watched for awhile, marveling, and then decided to go back into my tent and record my observations in a notebook. But as soon as I hit the sack and got out my notebook, I fell fast asleep again (this almost never happens; once I am up, I am up), and began to dream. *Vividly.* In my dream I was sitting at the entrance to my tent talking, as usual, to a group of Daribi friends. At the edge of my vision I saw a human-sized RAVEN (the American Northwest Coast *Bringer of Daylight*) leaning against a fence-post and eyeing me speculatively. Then, in a flash (POP—craack) *I* was leaning against the fencepost, watching my own body sitting and talking to my friends at the tent. And RAVEN was perched on my shoulders, with its wings upraised, *pouring light into the back of my head*. Like a Bringer of Daylight figure-ground reversal."

Coyote: "You damn fool, that was no lucid dream. That was what the Hindus call a *darsan*, a vision of the vision of your vision."

Roy: "Oh, you mean like *luck in the double focus*—like, for instance, a sonnet? RAVEN had assumed the classic position—shoulders and back of the head—of a possessing *izibidi* spirit in Daribi shamanic lore, a Lore-*bidi*. I got up from my *darsan* and out of my tent to tell someone about it, and found a group of Daribi women seated on the ground outside. When I told them my dream, one of them said, 'Now that is interesting. I just woke up myself, and had the same dream.' She had dreamt that she was sitting on the ground, talking to a circle of Daribi women in front of a house, when a tall, black man approached her, walked behind her, grabbed her by the hair, and pulled her head backward."

Coyote: "Like a bringer-of-*night*light figure-ground reversal."

Roy: "Exactly. But you see, by the Daribi reckoning of dream-imagery, this would be a portent of shamanic initiation."

Coyote: "So what was going on here? Why the substitution of a Native American power-vision for the blackbird that had invoked human mortality, while nearby a native Daribi vision of equivalent portent, the *darsan* of a *darsan*, indexing a normally prohibited crossing of the gender?

Roy: "The circumstances of my arrival, if not the Karimui landscape itself, gave a clue. As I was busy setting up my tent, the last of my earlier Daribi 'informants' (more of an intellectual *soul-brother*)—the wily, inscrutable Yapenugiai—lay dying in one of the nearby hamlets. This was the man who had originally told me about the *kauweri* and the curse of human mortality. I had been told he was very ill, but not much more, and should have drawn my own conclusions. He was already dead by the time I got to him, his body placed at the center of the cleared longhouse, with the gender-partition removed. There was a circle of mourners all around the edges. I did what I must: sat down next to him and cried over his body, keening in the Daribi fashion until my body was wracked by heaving sobs (one does not cry without *singing* in Daribi). *Farewell to him and farewell to a part of myself.*"

Coyote: "*Farewell to yesterday's tomorrow!*"

Roy: "But when I had finished *there was a problem.* How to take leave of those other mourners, *most of whom I did not know,* and many of whom, like Yapenugiai himself, had 'converted' (if that is the word) to a form of fundamentalist Christianity"?"

Coyote: "What to do, what to say?"

Roy: "Thinking quickly, I got to my feet, looked around the circle of mourners, and intoned the Oglala Lakota blessing that Wallace Black Elk had taught me, with its Daribi-like terminal nasal sound: AHO ME TA KWEASIN(g). "ALL OUR RELATIONS. Stunned silence! I turned on my heel and got out."

Coyote: "Any bets on where the RAVEN came from, or the double-vision of the RAVEN and kauweri? You're lucky they didn't Sioux you."

Roy: They couldn't—they were all my *relations.* As to the *bets,* the two blackbirds came from the same place Yapenugiai had gone to. And that was the first time anything like that had been reported from New Guinea, much less intimated in a vision."

Coyote: "What, binocular blackbird-watching? Intercontinental Ballistic Missives?"

Roy: "Nope, a total subject/object shift, or complete figure-ground reversal between knower and known, a sort of acute terraforming of the deceased Big Man, what Daribi call the *buruhoa.*"

Coyote: "What do the Sioux call it?"

Roy: "The *Custer Massacre.* Or, more politely, 'Rubbing out Long Hair.'"

Coyote: "Wait a minute, Roy, let us not confuse one form of ex-personation with another. Was this at about the time *the* magistrate was enlightening you about the mysteries of the *animating* principle?"

Roy: "As a matter of fact it was. Just about the time of Yapenugiai's death, or shortly thereafter."

Coyote: "And don't you see the connection?"

Roy: "As a matter of fact I did—it was a blackbird. I *think*."

Coyote: "So what, exactly, is a *buruhoa*?"

Roy: "During my earlier fieldwork I had confused the term with *buru-hwa*, the word for 'machete,' or bushknife. Though someone did say it was 'a kind of spirit.'"

Coyote: "Don't *change the subject*. What does *buruhoa* mean?"

Roy: "Well, *buru*, that means a *place*; *ho* means a 'whistle' or *ghost*; and-*a* is a sort of nominalizing suffix."

Coyote: "So, it means a *place-ghost*. And how did they tell you about it?"

Roy: "One guy, pointing at a peak of Mt. Karimui, said, 'You see that peak over there, the one they call Kebinugiai (e.g., 'Named For the Cassowary')? Well, that was once a man by that name, a great hunter who knew the land intimately well, by hunting on it all of his life. And when he died, he *became* that piece of land.' Expersonation and impersonation *simply change places*."

Coyote: "So, in other words, when *I* die, being a famous *trickster* and all . . . "

Roy: "When *you* die, Coyote, someone is going to say, 'You see that *roadkill* over there? Well, that was once a mangy *canid* who *asked too many questions*.'"

Coyote: "What? No 'And flights of RAVENS sing thee to thy rest?'"

Roy: "Nope, them RAVENS are just gonna come circling back and eat those scrawny yellow berries you use for eyes."

Coyote: "Look, Roy, you *assume* that Daribi Big Men, like this 'cassowary' guy, or Yapenugiai, turn into part of the landscape when they die. You *infer* that human beings can turn into a form of real estate when they die, but you have no real evidence. What CONCRETE evidence do you have that someone can go down like that?"

Roy: "The Mafia."

Coyote: "That only pertains to *water*, and *footwear*."

Roy: "The birds. The principle spiritual attainment by which the

buruhoa asserts his precedence over his former hunting bud-
dies, which happens to be very *traumatic*, something like
Genaro's *dreaming double*."

Coyote: "You mean like Schieffelin's eloquent book title: *Like People You See in a Dream?*"

Roy: "*In your* dreams, Coyote. I mean like *dreams you see in
people*."

Coyote: "Hey, Roy, didn't you just do that, with the *woman*, I
mean?"

Roy: "Nope, Yapenugiai did it all. You see, he was turning into a
buruhoa, and wanted to show his stuff, as a last gift to me. Because that is exactly what a *buruhoa* can do. It all goes to that
stuff we were saying about the eye not belonging to the body,
and the *picture-soul* of the person. See, game animals have picture-souls just as people do—'all our relations,' as the Lakota
would say. Everything *that moves of its own accord*, every *animate being*, has to have a projective, or *artificially separable* image to reconnoiter *with*, and *from*. *Know thyself* is one thing, a
mere platitude in the mouth of Polonius. Know *from* thyself is
the imperative of motion."

Coyote: "And that's what the *buruhoa* does, isn't it? The proof of
his being and nonbeing at one and the same time. The *secret*
of the *buruhoa*: he *separates* the picture-soul, or self-projective
body image of the game animal from the carcass, and sends it to
a hunter, in his dreams at night. He sends it as a *gift* to the hunter, just as Yapenugiai sent the *buruhoa* as his last gift to you."

Roy: "Sure, it's like the Native Americans say: the animal must *give*
itself to you, before you can successfully hunt it."

Coyote: "And that's why a Daribi hunter will suddenly wake up,
grab his bow and arrows, and run out into the woods, even in
the middle of the night. *He had a dream / the dream had him.*
And when he gets to the animal, he finds it stunned and disoriented without its self-image, and easy to kill."

Roy: "Every part of the landscape around Karimui was once a wily
and sagacious hunter, like Yapenugiai. Daribi say that when any
creature dies, its picture-soul can be seen hanging around the

place of death for a long time—*pragmatic afterlife*. But only a great hunter—and Yapenugiai was a great hunter—of myths, of shadows, of sorcery, *and* of anthropologists—can turn that pragmatic afterlife into the *very ground of being, terra firma—the picture of the hunter as the chase and the picture of the chase as the hunter*. No myth ever knows its place, unless that place also knows the myth-folk LORE/LORE folk—and it was Yapenugiai himself who first told me the secret of *Souw*, the *t'o nigare bidi*, or *maker of the land*, and his adventure with the *kauweri* bird."

Coyote: "And it was Yapenugiai himself who accompanied you on your quest for the meaning of the Daribi *habu* rite. Remember the domestication of the ghost, or human expersonation? When a human being dies, unmourned in the bush, his soul, or *bidinoma* is apt to turn *wild* and go around killing pigs and children for spite. And the *habu* is done to de-impersonate him as a human being."

Roy: "*Moving in a sacred manner*. You know, I once tried to record the life-story of Yapenugiai. You know, the kind of self-subjective *biography* that anthropologists are supposed to write: 'The Life and Times of a *Buruhoa*.'"

Coyote: "Sure, 'A long night's journey into day.'"

Roy: "More like 'Night of the Long Knives.' See, the details of his *personal* life were so *appalling* they could never be put into a book like this; they were *unprintable*."

Coyote: "Well, you *do* do *sonnets*, don't you?"

Roy: "Not this time. But the real problem was that he kept getting into *secrets* about things that he had experienced, or found out, secrets that were so mind-blowing that they stopped me cold in my tracks. I could have, and actually *did* write whole articles and books about each and every one of them, and I never did complete his life story."

Coyote: "That was *his* job, wasn't it? It is what the *kauweri* came back to tell you about. And in spite of that, you never did get all of those secrets down, did you?"

Roy: "Well, then they wouldn't be *secrets* anymore, would they?"

Coyote: "No, but without *secrets* there would be no anthropology.

Like, when there are no secrets anymore the anthropologist has to go and make them up."

Roy: "No way, Coyote, we do not have time for trivia like that. We make up *secrets* about secrets."

Coyote: "Like *word games make us proud to die*, eh? Like those *four undisclosed secrets* that, as the Daribi used to tell the white men around the station, 'the white man will never learn.' Tell me, Roy, is the *habu* one of those secrets? Is the origin myth one of those secrets, or the *buruhoa*, or the dreaded *keberebidi*?"

Roy: "How the hell should I know?"

Coyote: "See?"

You Tell the Secret / It Tells on You

Roy: "In a very crucial sense, knowledge and secrecy are reciprocals, they are inversely related. There is no knowledge without the secret, and so of course there are no secrets without knowledge. There are no cultures, only secrets, and there are no secrets, either, without the secret of the secret."

Coyote: "So what is the secret of the secret?"

Roy: "I'd tell you, but then I'd have to kill you. You don't know much about my family, do you?"

Coyote: "Well, we were coyotes, all down the line, plus or minus the odd wolf, some of which are very odd indeed."

Roy: "My dad was trained by the FBI, and our only other male in that generation was a CIA agent all his life."

Coyote: "And so *you* are what is known as a 'Sweeper,' strictly COUNTER-intelligence, if you know what I mean. So what *is* the difference between knowledge and secrecy?"

Roy: "POWER, pure, raw, naked power, the only thing the anthropologist has ever been interested in."

Coyote: "If that is the case, Mr. Counterintelligence, then why are anthropologists so powerless?"

Roy: "Because they tell their secrets, and then their secrets tell on them, and so, of course, *everybody* wants to kill them.

Coyote: "So why aren't the anthropologists already dead?"

Roy: "Most of them are, in one way or another. But then, of course, their enemies and detractors have a secret or two up their sleeves as well."

Coyote: "In other words, they have power."

Roy: "Sure, they kill them with kindness, they kill them with words, they kill them with sonnets, they kill them with . . ."*birds*. Like that wonderful secret Steve Feld discovered among the Kaluli. 'To you they are birds,' the Kaluli told him, 'to us they are voices in the forest.' Or perhaps *picture-souls*, as with Yapenugiai and the *buruhoa*."

Roy: "Or like that wonderful secret that Tony Crook discovered among the Bolivip, the one that the Bolivip high school student told him about: 'The old men always talk that way, they *change the subject in midsentence*. By the time you finish your work among us, all of our knowledge will be as a single sentence to you.'"

Coyote: "Why, that's the subject/object shift, Don Juan's Gimmick, the *dèjá vu* and *vùjá de*. By the time the 'old men' are done with you, or Don Juan, or Yapenugiai, or the sonnet, you will be convinced that the world is full of secrets, that culture is nothing but secrets, that there is one secret that explains everything . . . "

Roy: "By that time the anthropologist is *hooked*, and anyone at all can have their way with them. You see, it *doesn't matter* whether there are any secrets there or not; the investigator will automatically generate them by virtue of their own curiosity and insight, and that data will, through no fault of its own, allow one to see just exactly what one wants to see."

Coyote: "Or else the anthropologist is *unhooked*, and the world really *is* full of secrets—secrets that keep themselves so well that no one in the world will ever figure them out. And that brings us to another wonderful secret, this time discovered by Jane Fajans, among the Baining people of east New Britain: a people who never either impersonate nor expersonate themselves, nor anything else either."

Roy: "The Baining had always been the 'odd people out' for New Guinea anthropologists, the people with no culture, no society, no secrets. For instance, Gregory Bateson did his initial field-work among the Baining; he worked with them for seventeen months, yet they simply *would not talk to him*. He said that they *broke his heart.*"

Coyote: "So the secret of the Baining is that *they have no secrets?*"

Roy: "Nope, the secret of the Baining is that *they're not telling.*"

Coyote: "So how did Jane discover the secret of why they are not telling?"

Roy: "*Working misunderstanding.* By *understanding* that the Baining take their taboos very seriously, and so, reciprocally, that their taboos also take them very seriously—you know, *you tell the secret / it tells on you.* Suppose someone has a taboo on something, like eating pork. If they tell someone about the taboo, then *the secret is out* and they *have already broken the taboo.*"

Coyote: "So nobody can ever *tell* anything about anything, since you can never tell who has a taboo against what and you don't want to go around getting people to rat on themselves, because that would not only break their taboo, or their hearts, but break their very *lives.*"

Roy: "Nope. It is not that simple; it is that nobody ever *must* tell anything about anything—the injunction against talking is not simply a linguistic modality among the Baining, it is a *cultural*, or, if you prefer, a noncultural IMPERATIVE. It is like Wallace Stevens said: 'Let be be finale of seem / The only emperor is the emperor of ice cream.'"

Coyote: "In other words, the *imperative* is the *opposite* of a taboo, and that's why so many New Guinea languages are chock full of imperative forms. Like Daribi, which has a whole paradigm of imperatives worked through their whole grammar and syntax. Like *eno gerude nage te tiriamo*: 'Before my eyes you shall not, in future, do that.'"

Roy: "It's like a *rainbow*: it stands before your eyes, it positively *invites* your eyes, and yet it is deadly perilous to *point at it.*"

Coyote: "Tell me about the rainbow."

Roy: "Tell it to the RAVENS, buddy."

Coyote: "So what is the secret of Daribi sociality, or communality, or whatever you call it."

Roy: "It's the thing that made Yapenugiai's life so appalling: the *instantly communicable, mass-hysteria* MANPOWER CASCADE. 'I always thought they were pussycats,' my former wife said, when one of these erupted right in front of our house. 'Now look at them. They are like DEMONS, killing each other!'"

Coyote: "Why have we not heard of this before?"

Roy: "Anthropologists are a sedate lot, relying on routines, interviews, and controlled interactions for their self-confidence, their *tonal*. And so most fieldworkers dismiss the cascade as myth, legend, or exaggeration. The normal thing is to treat it statistically or medically, call it 'violence,' and make up some kind of sociological excuse for why it happens."

Coyote: "What's it like to be *in* one?"

Roy: "Like the biggest adrenaline rush you could ever imagine; scary as hell, but like a communal chained *orgasm*. I don't think 'violence' quite cuts it. Victor Turner's *communitas* is a bit closer, but the ancient Hindu *divine madness* or the early Teutonic WUT (pronounced 'voot') would be closest of all. Think of the dance of Kali; think of *pure abandon!*"

Coyote: "Is that what they mean by 'loose structures in Papua New Guinea, or symbolic constructions of reality? Like, I mean, *screw-loose*? 'The world is out of joint(s), O cursed spite / that ever I was born to set it right'? Like whenever things reach an intolerable degree of ambiguity, *it* happens?"

Roy: "Hamlet would be right at home there; the Viking *berserkers* would be *proud*. Robert Gardner caught it a few times in his magnificent film on the Dani DEAD BIRDS—the Dani call it *hunuk palin*. Merlin and Rumsey got it down perfectly, working with subjects in the Nabilya Valley who had gone back to tribal warfare. *The definition of a highlands social group is forever contingent.*"

Coyote: "What does that mean to you, Roy, or the Daribi"

Roy: "It means that *nagual* masquerades as *tonal*, dressed as its *own shadow*, just as the Magistrate said. It puts on the all-black body covering, with a black cassowary plume, that Daribi call the *ogwanoma*,' or boy-soul,' that would make people lose control of their bowels when they come upon it unawares. Then *all hell breaks loose!*"

Coyote: "Did you ever see it?"

Roy: "Many times; like, I *live with it*. In June 2000, I came out of my tent one morning to see a bearded young man complaining bitterly to Pusi, the village councillor. All his household gear had been ripped off during the night by some Chimbu bandits, who are called 'rascals' and hang out in the bush."

Coyote: "And the police were Chimbus, too, so they were of no help."

Roy: "As Pusi was explaining to him. And so I walked over to them and asked them if they had ever heard of *vigilantes*, explaining what I meant."

Coyote: "So then what happened?"

Roy: "Half an hour later the news came down: the bearded young man was *dead*. Returning to his hamlet he had confronted the first opponent he could find, a Daribi of the opposing faction. Venting his wrath upon him, he struck him repeatedly on the breastbone with the butt of his machete (*buruhwa*) to make his points. And the opponent drew his bow and shot him straight through the heart at point-blank range."

Coyote: "Wow! When these guys lose it, they *really lose it*. The Irish would be proud—like Rebecca of Donnybrook Farm, (sings): 'Not only did she do them *wrong*, she also did all of them *in*, them *in*, them *in* . . . '"

Roy (humoring him): " . . . and occasional pieces of skin, of skin, of skin.'"

Coyote: "So what happened then?"

Roy: "*All hell broke loose*, they touched off the MANPOWER CASCADE; all of the line of the dead man *and their friends* ran ululating through the community, burning the houses and despoiling the gardens of the opposing faction and driving them into permanent exile in the bush. And *then* it began: all the roads for miles around were choked with mourners, coming in to vent their grief over the body. They wailed for days and nights, nonstop, smashing the possessions of the people living there, cutting down their fruit trees, despoiling *their* gardens, *because they did not take care of him.*"

Coyote: "And you could barely make it down to the station, even to leave Karimui—down through the lines of mourners, and the mud, and the incessant La Niña rain of that year. To wait for your plane for days, which could not make it because of the weather. And you, after the *secret* of Daribi sociality."

Roy: "*Let me point out,* Coyote, that my leaving Karimui always had to do with *rainbows.*"

Coyote: "There you go again, Roy, pointing at things you should not. Tell me now: did you ever *not* make a mistake in your whole *life?*"

Roy (somewhat abashed): "Well, I was *born . . .*"

Coyote: "Sure, you were *born,* everybody was *born. I* was born. Shucks, even Yapenugiai was born . . ."

Roy: "Let me *finish,* dammit. I was born in what is clinically known as the *double-breech presentation:* ass-backward and up-side-down, with the navel cord wrapped around my neck!"

Coyote: "Well that, at least, explains your *sonnets.* What it does *not* explain, besides of course *rainbows,* is the *origin* of things: how the Daribi got to *be* that way. Not only the manpower cascade, but the whole friggin' *world-view* of how *things* got to be that way."

Roy: "*Explanation,* Coyote, is a very dirty game, sometimes rising to the level of a *blood-sport.*"

Coyote (sings): ". . . and occasional pieces of *skin,* of *skin,* of *skin . . .*"

The Secret of Daribi Holography:
The Pearlshell, the Self-Modeling Series,
the Manpower Cascade, and the Keberebidi

Roy: "Remember our friend the Magistrate, the shadow-catcher, the one who showed me the source of my own animation?"

Coyote: "Roy, that was *your* revelation, not his; he only *helped.*"

Roy: "Well, in that case I needed some further help, having just made another discovery myself—that of the truly *holographic* world perspective, *dramatically enacted,* of the Barok people of New Ireland. I wanted to know whether the Daribi had anything like that."

Coyote: "And you asked him, didn't you, you *born-again mistake in sonnet's clothing*?"

Roy: "No, I *showed* him. Night after night (for he was sleeping in the doorway of my tent to protect me from rascals) I showered him with the most vivid examples of holographic worldviews in other parts of New Guinea. Not only mine, among the Barok but also Jadran Mimica's, is, among the Jeghuye, Arve Sørum's among the Bedamini, even Gillian Gillison's among the neighboring Gimi people. After a while he could rehearse them in his sleep."

Coyote: "So what did he say to all of that"?"

Roy: "Not much. The *perfect mutual occlusion of part and whole in any human contingency* is a damn hard thing to *think* about, much less talk about. Like when I asked Louis Dumont whether he realized he had created anthropology's first holographic model in his book on the Hindu caste system, *Homo Hierarchicus,* he said, 'Holo . . . what?'"

Coyote: "Quit hedging, Roy; what did the *magistrate* say?"

Roy: "He said, 'I am dead sure we have one of these; I just can't think of what it is.'"

Coyote: "So what is it, the *manpower cascade*?"

Roy: "*In a manner of speaking.* All significant Daribi mythology and symbolism—origin myth, sorcery practice, even marriage and kinship—are based on a three-sided metaphorical synthesis. The word *ge* in Daribi means both 'pearlshell' and 'egg.'"

Coyote: "Like pearlshell, the traditional *icon* of Daribi *vital wealth*, the archetypal *signifier* in bride-price, child-price, and death exchanges, is the immortal *picture-soul* of human mortality. Pearlshells are the human 'eggs' that never hatch, but keep being traded for human life potential, moving opposite, in the necessary exchanges, to the flow of human life and procreation. *Human beings are mortal beings with immortal eggs*."

Roy: "*Got it in one*, you *bloodhound*. Whereas *birds* are mortal beings with *mortal* eggs: they hatch out of their eggs, their eggs hatch of them, they hatch again out of their eggs, and so it goes, in a never-ending cycle. We move *parallel* to our eggs, they move through them, and vice-versa."

Coyote: "Got it in *two*, you bloody *Anti-twin*. So what about the magical, if not only symbolic, third-order *synthesis*? Or, as you would call it, the *obviation*?"

Roy: "*Snakes*, however, *are* the magical, third-order synthesis. For although snakes also lay eggs, the snake, after hatching out of its egg, *keeps hatching out of itself*, shedding its skin over and over, and so forever renewing its youth. *Snakes are immortal beings with mortal eggs*."

Coyote: "So the series is completed, or, as you would say, *obviated*: triple play—pearlshell on first, hatchling on second, and then to *immortality*, back on home plate. But as that is only a *game*—a metaphor, or dramatization of a purely symbolic truth. How does it relate to the manpower cascade, or the deadly keberebidi sorcery?"

Roy: "In other words, what is to keep Louis Dumont from saying 'Holo-what?' all over again. Like Yogi Berra's *déjà vu*. Well, look, Mr. Dawgnabbit, I got your 'hollow what' *right here*."

Coyote: "What, another *Cleveland Indians fastball*, like back in '48?"

Roy: "Not this time, Feller. It has to do with the *self-modeling series*, of which the snake is only an *impersonation*, and with the secret of Daribi mathematics—the fact that there are only three *necessary numbers*—there is no such thing as *strike four*."

Coyote: "I thought *all numbers* were necessary."

Roy: "Nope, they just *do not count.* The Daribi, I mean. Or at least they did not, before the introduction of Tokpisin, the New Guinea *lingua franca* ('French kiss,' for those who do not speak the language). Traditional Daribi mathematics was not based on *counting,* that is, placing numbers in a one-to-one correspondence with an appropriate collection of *countables.* Nor was it based on the remapping of number upon number, what we call 'number theory'—addition, subtraction, multiplication, and division."

Coyote: "So, in other words, they *had no mathematics* in our sense."

Roy: "True, and what is worse, *we* have no mathematics in their sense, either. Daribi mathematics is based on a peculiar ratio established between *duality,* or *scission,* with itself, and its only comparative feature is that ratio itself, called *sidari-si,* the 'two-together-two.'"

Coyote: "Like the Anti-twins, gender and laterality, and like *déjà vu* and *vùjá de,* impersonation and expersonation playing games with each other."

Roy: "Eggs-actly. The word *si* means either 'two' or 'half,' and usually both at the same time. So *si-dari-si* could mean anything from 'one fourth' to 'four,' or any fractional or multiplicative derivative of the comparative process one might wish to pursue. It could even mean *si* taken to the power of *si,* provided only that we could figure out what power that was."

Coyote: "So what's the *bottom line?*"

Roy: "The bottom line is that *sidari-si* automatically cancels out the possibility of *even numbers,* which are like birds reproducing themselves endlessly—and *thereby also excludes the possibility of numeri-comparisons!* ANY numerical comparisons."

Coyote: "What about the *snake,* the automatically self-modulating series?"

Roy: "That, my friend, is why the Daribi had *only three numbers— deri, si,* and *sera.*'"

Coyote: "Que será será?"

Roy: "Precisely: *got it in three,* the *third-order synthesis!* See, the first two numbers of a self-modeling series are *stochastic*, self-indeterminate, like the *binaries* used in computers. And that is because the first two numbers, or points of origination, in such a series *do not yet* constitute a series in themselves, given the formula n + 1 = n + n-1, which cannot come *into its own* until the third term is reached. And after that it is unbeatable, like a manpower cascade."

Coyote: "So, in other words, computers are *for the birds*."

Roy: "And Daribi are for the snakes. Our most familiar example of a self-modeling series is the Fibonacci series, which begins 0, 1, 1, 2, 3, 5, 8, 13, ... but, depending on the first two numbers, it *could* be, with a wide variety of other possible options."

Coyote: "But why is a self-modeling series unbeatable?'"

Roy: "Because it is made of its own interference-patterning, or modeled upon the interference-patterning of a single series with itself, like the *linearly coherent, nonradiating beam of a laser-projection*. And like the HOLOGRAPHIC image projected by that beam, which is not so much symbolic as it is *scientific*; an *image that stands for itself*."

Coyote: "Wait a minute, Hoy. You're telling me that that image could be the *ogwanoma*', the Daribi *boy-soul*, generated by the interference-patterning of disruptive factionalism, foolhardy bravado."

Roy: "Coyote, I'm not telling you *anything*, I'm *showing* you. Because the intervals between the numbers, or successive members, are taken up as the values of the numbers themselves, after a brief lapse of time (anticipating self, nagual, *anticipates* recollective self, tonal, is *per Don Juan*), the *internal cohesion* or intimate *self-contagion* of the sequence *substitutes itself for time itself* and carries the day. It *dominates* by dominating itself."

Coyote: "So a *sonnet* that based its *acoustical meaning* on a self-interfering rhyme-scheme pattern would take precedence over any other sonnet."

Roy: "I thought you had already figured that out. It would merge with its own imagery, become *part of its own reality*."

Coyote: "Then a lovely young women, somewhat disenchanted,

falling from 6,000 feet without the aid of a parachute would likewise merge with her own reality."

Roy: "Provided she was *well-cushioned* and she acted with *pure abandon*, like those Daribi warriors."

Coyote: "And a *weapon*, based on that principle, could dominate any other wavetrain, and blind any radar or any other sensory or computorial equipment on the battlefield."

Roy: "Goes without saying; it could wipe out computer-memory or, if powerful enough, bring *ordinary* memory, which is based on brain waves, to a standstill. Remind me to write you an *immemorial* sonnet."

Coyote: "*Merging with its own reality* reminds me of the *echidna*, the New Guinea anteater-monotreme *Zaglossus*, whose brain lacks a *hippocampus* or organ of long-term memory and so, as you once put it, it *walks forever in the daylight of the now*, in a *dream* of itself. And it *also lays eggs*."

Roy: "Funny you should remember that; most of its victims don't. *Zaglossus* is the secret of the dreaded *keberebidi* 'memory-wipe' sorcery, the agency to which Daribi have traditionally attributed *all deaths*."

Coyote: "What? And not to the manpower-cascade?"

Roy: "It's practically the same thing. Researchers have just discovered that *Zaglossus* has a *bioelectric* antenna in its long curving snout, one that by all evidence must project a self-modulating electronic impulse, one that acts to dissipate the self-orienting body image of its prey, *just like the buruhoa*. After which it simply grabs the ants and eats 'em."

Coyote: "So how does it get involved with sorcery?"

Roy: "By means of a *ruse*, likewise connected with the *egg*. See, the word *keberebidi* is taken to mean 'cassowary-man,' suggesting the stealth of that mysterious bird whose plumage is used to embellish the *ogwanoma*.' But in fact it does not; *kebi* or *tori* is the word for 'cassowary' whereas *kebere* is based on an archaic Daribi usage: *ge-bere*, meaning 'egg-hider' or 'egg-concealer.'"

Coyote: "So how does the sorcery work?"

Roy: "I'd tell ya, but then I'd have to kill ya. That's the way the Daribi treat it—'What makes you think I have anything to do with anything so evil,' etc. *Nobody* knows how it is done, so *everybody* finds out. It is actually quite simple. A raiding party of *kebere-bidi* finds a lone victim, knocks him unconscious, and plays the *kebere-ge* across the victim's thorax, wiping out all memory of the event. That makes the victim disoriented, without his memory-image of himself and, when the lone assassin comes to dispatch him, quite easy to kill."

Coyote: "What is the *kebere-ge*, and where does it come from?"

Roy: "From 'places that have white-limestone outcrop,' according to the Daribi; they find them in limestone caves beneath that outcrop. Shucks, even *kids* know about it. Looking through my early field notes I found the following entry, told to me by some Daribi children in December, 1963: 'Small *keberebidi* hatch from eggs that are covered with spines.'"

Coyote: "And then, in May, 1964:

Some women of Masi were walking around the gardens of Maina and saw the footprints of a man. They followed them to a hole in the base of a tree. Here they found some dry grass and banana leaves, and underneath them the *kebere-ge*. This was furry, and had a nose, but no feet, eyes, or ears. A vine was tied around it in the shape of a U.

Roy: "Finally, in December 1968:

Oza is a place where the *keberebidi* was obtained. The mountain was broken on top, and the "children" of the *keberebidi* fall down from the mountain. The *kebere-ge* is the child of the sorcery. They are like fruit; some fall on the ground, some fall on trees. People who are quiet and stealthy picked them up. The sorcery is found where the stone is all white (e.g., limestone), inside the broken stone. The *kebere-ge* is like a stone. One of the people in a *kebere* raid carries the *kebere-ge* in a *bilum* (net bag). When the victim is "killed," the *keberebidi* recites a spell (*pobi*), touches the *ge* to the thorax, and resurrects the victim.

The *kebere-ge* hides the marks of violence, and when the victim returns to his house the episode is erased from his memory. His mind is confused. People say that the *kebere-ge* is "half living, and half inanimate."

Coyote: "Roy, none of this makes any sense until one realizes the profound significance that the Daribi attach to eggs, mortality, and immortality. Daribi call the embryo a 'child-egg,' *wai-ge*, and they call the net bag (*bilum*) in which an infant is carried a 'pouch' (*sagau*), like that of a marsupial. Or, for that matter, a monotreme."

Roy: "And none of that made any sense either until the expert on Australasian wildlife, Tim Flannery, came to Charlottesville and confirmed some of my suspicions about *Zaglossus sp.*"

Coyote: "What, he discovered that *you* were a *kebere-ge*?"

Roy: "Nope, he told me that *Zaglossus* does have a dormancy period of about a month and a half."

Coyote: "So then it might seek the shelter of a limestone cave to wait out its dormancy period, and the wet drip from the rocks would cover its spiny body with a calcite solution, which would then harden, giving the appearance of an anomalous 'thing' that was half animate and half inanimate."

Roy: "But the real *scientific* solution to the sorcery would be that the bioelectric antenna in its snout would carry a residual charge, enough that, when deployed suitably and played across the thorax of a victim, it would dissipate the self-orienting body image of the victim."

Coyote: "And thus have the effect of a post-hypnotic death suggestion, like the 'vibrating hand' that the martial arts people talk about. You know, first you deliver a seemingly innocuous blow, weakening the *chi* of the victim. Then, when the victim is lulled into a false sense of security, the martial artist delivers a second blow to the already weakened *chi*, and death results. Just exactly like the *keberebidi*."

Roy: "Or like a *buruhoa*, or a miniaturized scale model *merging with its own reality* of the *manpower cascade*."

Coyote: "Roy, the Daribi taught you well. Once you get your act down pat, you go looking for someone to kill."

Roy: "*Not necessarily*, Coyote. As the Daribi say, '*a child is a wound from within*.' Notwithstanding the sad facts of my birth, one of the moments of pure joy in my life was discovering that I have the same birthday as Mahatma Gandhi, Wallace Stevens, and Groucho Marx."

Coyote: "See what I mean? Tell 'em Groucho sent ya. Welcome to our show, *Crypto Marx*. Come on, now, *bore us all from within*."

Roy: "Merging with one's own reality is no joke. There is a medieval French epitaph that goes: 'Before he lived only for others; now he lives only for himself.'"

Coyote: "*Pure narcissism* is the basic personality structure of our times; totally self-absorbed and totally self-destructive at the same time. Like, 'it may *seem* boring from the outside, but once you get down to the inner core, you realize that it is *deadly* boring.'"

Roy: "*Expersonation* is like the Daribi manpower cascade: it is only dangerous when you *think* you know what it is."

Coyote: "Like a shopping mall, or like a R A I N B O W."

Chasing Rainbows

Roy: "It's back to the *buruhoa*, and the Cessna, and the *story of my life*. You know, I luck in the double focus.

Coyote: "DUMB luck!"

Roy: "Nope. *Scintillating* luck. See, when I left Karimui, after my first fieldwork, this time in a *twin* Cessna, a DOUBLE RAIN-BOW formed around the plane and paced our flight, all the way to Goroka. And the Daribi with me, they were *pissing* scared."

Coyote: "You mean *pissing rainbows*?"

Roy: "No *such luck*, they are a very careful people. And then, when I was coming back to Karimui for the *second* time, I had some trouble getting my research permit."

Coyote: "Don't tell me: it was made out in *triplicate*?"

Roy: "Nice *try*. Nope, I was driving through Wyoming, on my way to Seattle, when a DOUBLE RAINBOW arced across the sky, straight in the direction of Seattle, as though marking it."

Coyote: "*Mark Twain*, Roy. And when you got to Seattle you discovered that the research permit had arrived there on the very same day that you saw the rainbow, and *at the precise hour* that you saw it in Wyoming."

Roy: "And it *goes on*. When my son was four years old, he surprised me one day by saying, 'Rainbows can steal ducks.' And I said, 'Don't be silly, Jonathan, how can a *rainbow* steal a *duck*?'"

Coyote: "And he said, 'Simple. It makes itself longer, comes down, and *grabs the duck*.' Or, you see, the *anthropologist*. Memory image, wound from within, expersonation, manpower cascade, *that* sort of thing."

Roy: "Oh, you must mean my *son's* son, little Graham, that day at the San Antonio Zoo."

Coyote: "It is the cutest thing in the world: every time Graham goes to the zoo he goes to the aquarium tank of his favorite grouper fish, and the two of them *kiss each other through the glass*."

Roy: "Mere *guppy love*. Not real *bird-flirting*, like with the *kauweri*. So I wandered over to the *aviary*, and there, in one of the cages, was a lovely young zoo attendant flirting with a RAINBOW LORY, the bird the Daribi call ABUPAGAI."

Coyote: "What does ABUPAGAI *mean*, in Daribi?"

Roy: "It means something so *awesome* it should never be put into words. But, etymologically, it translates as 'father-based,' or 'father-filled.'"

Coyote: "So it *really* means something, like '*Duck*, big daddy is coming.'"

Roy: "You must never point at pretty girls, Coyote; they might take you for a *bird-dog*."

Coyote: "And you must never point at RAINBOWS, either, at least if you are a Daribi."

Roy: "Nor if you are an ancient Chinese person, either. There is a line in the Chinese *Book of Songs*, the Confucian classic, that goes, 'There is a RAINBOW in the east; no one dares to *point at* it.'"

Coyote: "So what is this thing about *pointing at* RAINBOWS, Roy?"

Roy: "Search me, research me, I wouldn't know it from my own grandson."

Coyote: "A long story, and a *wet* one."

Roy: "Sure. Still *wet behind the ears*, on my first independent journey around Karimui, I saw a fleeting RAINBOW in the sky at a place called Nekapo. There was a group of older Daribi men sitting on the ground, ostensibly gathered to talk to me, or *something*. I asked them what it was, and most likely *pointed* at it."

Coyote: "*Dead silence*. Lots of *muttering*. Like, 'These guys claim to have invented *powered flight*, something crazy like that, and *there he stands, pointing* . . . like he's at the *San Antonio Zoo* or something.'"

Roy: "Hell of a lot *they* knew about *grandsons*. Then one of them broke the silence and said it was an *unigibidi*, and that an *unigi* was a kind of iridescent *snake*."

Coyote: "Well, from now on I'll know where to go for real disinformation, like in Cleveland, where they don't just *fore*cast the weather, they OVERcast it."

Roy: "And then there was the time that Suabe and his family invited me to name their newborn son."

Coyote: "And you suggested ABUPAGAI, didn't you, And *they* turned around and ran like hell."

Roy: "Give 'em a break, Coyote, they were from Dobu, the homeplace of ABUPAGAI."

Coyote: "Didn't need you to *point them out*, hey?"

Roy: "Nope, too *disappointing*. Meanwhile, back at the ranch, Tultul Hanari told me of a Daribi folk-belief: If you point at a RAINBOW, your mother's breasts will burst. Then he laughed and said, 'My mother is already dead, so I can point at all the RAINBOWS I want.'"

Coyote: "And when he had recovered he explained to you that the so-called folk-belief was just a simple deception, of 'the stork brought you' kind, designed to fool small children and keep them from POINTING AT RAINBOWS."

Roy: "DAMN STRAIGHT MISTER. There is often profound wisdom in these so-called simple folk-beliefs, like the Daribi counterintelligence about the airplane: The white man has just invented a new kind of airplane, that doesn't need any wings at all, but can travel the whole way along the ground, where it *really matters!*"

Coyote: "See, Roy, every culture has its *say* things, things that one normally says, about *everything*. Even scholars have their say in things, and, like Don Juan says, 'They spend all day running through their inventory, *competitively*, with one another, and then, when 5 o'clock comes around, they go home and try to forget it.'"

Roy: "But what my friend Badu Buruhwa, the Daribi doctor who runs the hospital, told me, which really *shook* me, was, 'Sure that story about Souw, the Maker of the Land, that is a great story. But the story of ABUPAGAI, that is truly *awesome*.'"

Coyote: "So tell me the story about ABUPAGAI."

Roy: "There isn't any story about ABUPAGAI; it would be too much like pointing at a rainbow."

Coyote: "Well, then tell me a *fragment*."

Roy: "That's funny, because that's just what I asked the magistrate, you know, that disenfranchised expert on holographic worldviews? He responded with a fragment about how Souw had invented the first *cow*."

Coyote: "Roy, *this is getting us nowhere*."

Roy: "Funny, too, because that is exactly what the *bull* said."

Coyote: "Roy, I know *pure bull* when I see it. Get on with the *fragment*."

Roy: "Okay this is what I got:

ABUPAGAI is the same as the *hoa-bidi* (*buruhoa*). ABUPAGAI, when he died, followed ("behinded") the rain and the lightning. He had a space behind the waterfall, and he died there. He died, and his bones were there. People came and saw them. When it thunders, ABUPAGAI FLIES ON TOP; his wings make the wind. When this happens in the morning, it will rain all day. ABUPAGAI makes it rain; he follows the lightning and thunder around.

Coyote: "Roy, it is plain as day just exactly what this means. It can't be a *bird*, because nothing was mentioned about a bird. And it can't be a waterfall, either, because, 'he left his bones behind the waterfall,' so it must be that thing that shimmers in front of a waterfall, if you tilt your head just right, and also FLIES ON TOP of a rainstorm, and nests, so to speak, in the cumulonimbus, forms around the lucky Cessna, announces research permits to weary travelers . . ."

Roy: "STOP RIGHT THERE, Coyote. You are perilously close to PERDITION; you are about to commit a NON-CARDINAL SIN!"

Coyote (going on, as though nothing had happened, which is, in fact, the case): "Whereas, if you so much as POINT YOUR FINGER AT IT, you will be struck, instantly, by *lightning*."

Roy: "There is not now, nor was there ever, a *Ben Franklin* at Karimui. And, in any case, *you haven't got the key*. The only thing this means is that if you go ahead and point it out, your MAMA will be SORREE."

Coyote: "Yet, nonetheless, the story goes on."

Roy: "DAMN STRAIGHT the story goes on. It was the ANTI-TWINS all along, and it goes on because ABUPAGAI had a grandson."

Coyote: "And his grandson was caught *smooching groupies* at the San Antonio Zoo."

Roy: "Nope, *wrong grandson*. ABUPAGAI'S grandson had *beetle-wings*, and was named DOBUBIDI, not Graham, and he was the founder of the sui generis Dobu lineage."

Coyote: "*Sui-generis*? You mean they came from PIGS?"

Roy: "Nope, that would be the curse of *sow*, not *Souw*. I mean they came from INCEST. That is the story of Dobubidi."

Coyote: "I don't follow."

Roy: "It's like the ANTI-TWINS would say: High levels of humor and incest signify only one thing: *extreme personal, social, and intellectual uncertainty, and a frustrated attempt to do something about it.*"

Coyote: "But that's *two* things!"

Roy: "Welcome to *reality* pardner; that's the ANTI-TWINS talking."

Coyote: "I smell another story."

Roy: "Dobubidi lived in the deep river-gorge country to the west of Karimui—sheer 3,000-foot cliffs, that sort of thing. He had taken a wife from the Mt. Ialibu region, where the Daribi say they came from. He and his wife had a daughter, and when the daughter grew up, Dobubidi began to cohabit with her. And his wife was *pissed*."

Coyote: "I would be *pissed* too."

Roy: "I mean *pissed off*. So she went back to her people at Ialibu and said, 'I married a MONSTER, you gotta *do* something about it.' So they raised an *army*, you know, touched off a *manpower cascade*, and the army marched down the river gorge toward Karimui to give Dobubidi *what for*."

Coyote: "So what did Dobubidi do about it?"

Roy: "Well, he ate a lot of sugarcane and left huge piles of *leavings* around, as though an immense number of men had been camping there. And then, when he saw the manpower cascade coming along the river gorge, he got on his *beetle-wings*. He unfolded the wings from under those glossy wing cases and flew to the top of one of those 3,000-foot precipices. 'Hey you guys over there,' he shouted, 'ARE YOU READY FOR THEM?' Then he flew to the top of another and called back "WE SURE ARE, HUNDREDS OF US, WHAT ABOUT YOU GUYS?' And he flew back and forth, calling like that, from one butte to another, until the whole place was echoing with his cries."

Coyote: "So what did those guys from Ialibu do about this?"

Roy: "They said to their daughter, 'Look, sweetie, we don't care what kind of MONSTER you married, WE'RE OUT OF HERE! You can do what you like: come with us, or go back and live with this pedophile.' So she went back and lived with

Dobubidi, and he begat the Dobu lineage upon his very own daughter."

Coyote: "So what is the *moral* of this story?"

Roy: "*If you've got it, FLAUNT it*! Actually the whole thing is a *cautionary tale* about the whole secret of Daribi sociality as well as sociopathy: the manpower cascade, the *keberebidi*."

Coyote: "The ANTI-TWINS. SIDARI-SI. OBVIATION. MERG-ING WITH ONE'S OWN REALITY."

Roy: "But not the RAINBOW, see? Only ABUPAGAI and his buggy *grandson*."

Coyote: "So it's back to square one: the *eye does not belong to he body* . . ."

Roy: "But the body itself, or perhaps the picture-soul, *belongs to its internal vibrations*—nerve-impulses, synaptic responses, breath-ing, blood-flow, *memory*, speech, gestures, impulsive action, the *active subject*. Plus the same periodicity that is used to *augment* those vibrations can also be used to *dampen* them. SHOUT IT FROM THE MOUNTAINTOPS!"

Coyote: "Call in the CAVALRY!"

Roy: "You got it:

We use a kind of leverage, the face,
the elbow-joints and knees, the pantomime
emotions of the heart, to make sublime
the patterned movements that our thoughts
erase, *to lift the tail and arch the neck of rhyme*,
use equine sweep and figure to make pace—
the borrowed muscles of the human race
forget themselves as language every time.

To flay the teeth with pheromones, to mate
convulvular the long and rolling gait,
the rigid back that liquefies the leather;
to sound the eunuch-horn, to make the noun
re-verb-erate, to take the wind in tether—
WHAT GOOD IS POETRY WHEN WRITTEN DOWN?

Coyote (sings, in German): *"Lory, lory, lory, lory, schön sind die Madchen von sechzehn, achtzehn Jahr"* "

Roy: *"Die Gegenzwillingen sind allmächtig,* Coyote: *word games make us proud to live!"*

Coyote: "Tell it to the guys at CalTech."

The Golden Section

Roy: "What? And give away the secret to Daribi ecology, gardening practice, community-building, the self-defining and self-destroying social unit? *Si deri teruwaiu,* 'making one of two,' the Golden-Sectioning of Daribi settlement pattering."

Coyote: "Don't tell me it's the manpower cascade all over again?"

Roy: "Well, that too, but this time in reverse: the *dampening effect* is also self-augmenting. Daribi call it *me bidigo ni gerigi-bizhu,* 'staying *en masse* to cut other peoples' garden.' They swarm, Coyote, they *pullulate*—all able-bodied men and boys comes together to cut the gardens of the whole community."

Coyote: "Like, when you first worked at Karimui, your community numbered about 200 souls, and now it's over 800."

Roy: "And the total population has increased from about 5,000 to over 20,000."

Coyote: "Wow, these guys breed like *rabbits.*"

Roy: "Rabbits do not cut gardens. They breed like *Daribi.*"

Coyote: "So tell me about the Golden Section."

Roy: "I'll show you about the Golden Section. Indigenous Karimui peoples do not live in isolated longhouses, scattered across the landscape, but rather like social insects, in *hives,* or compact *unities.* They swarm. That is the secret of how the hive is formed: it both generates and distributes itself, following the radial drainage pattern—some of them expanding and merging, others forming or dispersing all by themselves (in some cases across rugged terrain.)"

Coyote: "Actually, it looks like a bad case of *hives* on the *non-*rainforest. And the Golden Section would be the *honey.*"

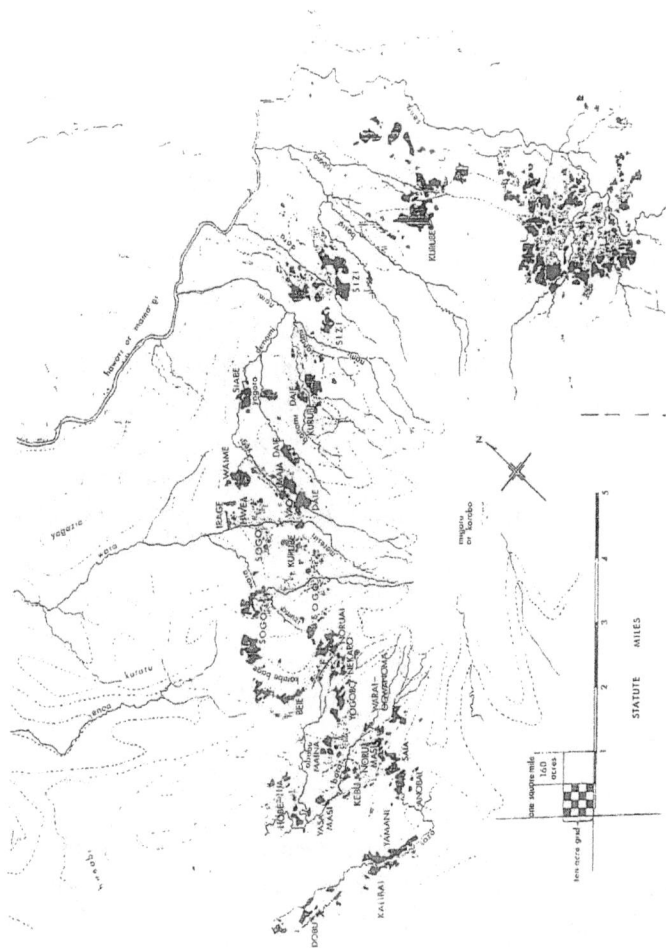

3. A Bad Case of Hives

Roy: "Let's keep our *Schatzele* to ourselves, even if they are named 'Lory.'"

Coyote: "So when Karimui people start to form a new community, it's like *homesteading*. They build their longhouses in a tight cluster, with the gardens around them. Then as the land tires out and the population expands, they move outward, cutting new gardens and building new houses on the periphery, forming an ever-expanding *ring* around the fallow land."

Roy: "And the people—they harry each other and they marry each other, forming unions across the lineage-boundaries, unions that are themselves people. So that yesterdays blood-and-marriage ties are tomorrow's kin-unities—deeds of a new lineage with boundaries of their own. And as the boundaries become people, so the people themselves become boundaries—all generated by the interference-patterning."

Coyote: "So the communities divide as they breed, and breed as they divide, like cells in the body. But where do the ANTI-TWINS come in?"

Roy: "That goes to the *conceptual* core of indigenous Daribi mathematics, the ratio formed by duality or scission with itself: *si-dari-si*. The only way in which the Daribi seem to be able to conceptualize the political or ideological aspects of the community process is by *twinning* the definable lineal units with one another through an idiom of intermarriage, sharing, and exchanging. Regardless of the other facts, they understand the process as a making and separating of *pairs*."

Coyote: "Whereas, as we have seen, the whole *dynamic* of the process—garden-cutting *bees*, manpower cascade, and even the insidious 'memory-deathray' of the *kebere-ge*—operate on the principle of the self-modeling series, a principle that can only come into its own, or 'synthesize' itself, once the magical three is reached. Is 'merging with its own reality' *out of consciousness* for the Daribi?"

Roy: "In fact they *have no name* for the thing or process that we have been objectifying as the 'community,' any more than bees have a name for the hive. It is *too important*, too much a part of its own *context*, like Freud's *subconscious*. Too *holographic*. How would you objectify the process of objectification itself?"

Coyote: "So the *phenomenal* essence, or *tonal*, of the Karimui community is a *Golden Section holography*, eh? How can that *bee*? Hadn't you ought to let us in on the secret of the Golden Section, Roy?"

Roy: "The Golden Section, the *phi* of the mathematicians, is, properly speaking, the *tonal* of shape, or shaping—the *proportioning* of *proportion* with itself. The best way to show this is a *linear* demonstration: you divide a line into three segments, asymmetrically, by making two cuts along it, *such that the smallest segment, at the one end, stands in the same relation to the medial segment, in the middle, as the two of them do to the largest segment, at the other end.*"

Coyote: "But Roy, that's your 'magical three,' the *third-term synthesis*, where the self-modeling series comes into its own, Daribi *sena*, in relation to the stochastic duality-ratio of scission with itself, Daribi *sidari-si*."

Roy: "Hence the *intimate relation* of the Golden Section's proportionality to the self-modeling series. If you form a series of ratios, or fractions, with the successive members of the Fibonacci series as the denominators, and the successive members of that same series, *stepped back by one*, as the numerators, *that series of ratios will approach the Golden Section as a limit as it approaches infinity*."

Coyote: "Sidari *three*, as it were. And because such a self-modeling series, manpower-cascade, or whatever models itself upon itself, taking up the numerical intervals between the number-values within the numbers themselves that follow them, *the Golden Section is implicit in the self-modeling series*."

Roy: "With all the properties, proportions, and vibrational values pertaining thereunto. There are many examples of this in nature, such as the growth and self-proportioning of the nautilus shell, or the growth and distribution of *flower petals*. Probably harmonics have something to do with it, as in the group-howling of *canids*."

Coyote: "And there are many examples of it in *culture*, too, particularly in architecture and design, such as the temples constructed by the ancient Egyptians, Minoans, and Greeks. Especially
the *labyrinths*. Tell me, why is that?"

Roy: "Because the self-modeling series has the special effect of
dominating all wave-trains but its own. And because *memory* is
made of waves, as in the case of the *kebere-ge*, *speech* is made of
waves, *thought* is made of waves, *vision* is made of waves, *radar*
is made of waves . . . COYOTES are made of waves, *earthquakes*
are made of waves. And also because the self-modeling series
has the effect of *dampening* or canceling out any wave-train that
is not of its ilk."

Coyote: "So, then, those outside of a Minoan labyrinth could
not hear the anguished cries of the hero battling the Minotaur
within."

Roy: "And for the same reason the labyrinth itself would be to
some degree earthquake-proof. Like the Parthenon in Athens,
or the Egyptian temples: any structure founded and constructed
upon the specifics of the Golden Section will model itself upon
the dampening effect and so sustain itself against the irregular
waves of seismic shock."

Coyote: "So what about that 'special effect' that the Golden Section
is most famous for: that anything modeled upon the Golden
Section or its proportions will appear *especially pleasing* to the
eye? Like the Parthenon, for instance?"

Roy: "Well, *vision* is made of waves, too, and the effect of the proportioning is to cancel out the irregularities of *insight* and *kill
'em with beauty* (always a matter of proportioning and interference-patterning). Real beauty is always very *lethal* and erosive of
the memory, as in: 'To drink from the waters of *Lethe*.'"

Coyote: "Didn't you call your first book on *obviation*, *Lethal
Speech*?"

Roy: "Sure did, and on the basis of obviation, and also the *kebere-ge*, you could *weaponize* anthropology, make a very nif-
ty military weapon by modeling an electronic pulse upon the

self-modeling series. It would blind radar, computers, and any sensory or electronic weapon on the battlefield, possibly even act upon the organisms of the soldiers themselves."

Coyote: "So there's hope for your sonnets yet!"

Roy: "Taste, Coyote, is also a matter of interference-patterning."

Coyote: "Still, Roy, there is a problem. Sure, the self-modeling series *interferes with itself*, acquires a spontaneity or self-mimetic originality all its own and *becomes its own criterion*, or standard of non-symbolic judgment. *Just as language does*. But, as per your example of the line divided into segments, or the Greco-Egyptian labyrinth, or, for that matter, the laser beam, *it does so in a strictly linear fashion*, even if it does take a spiral form, like the nautilus shell."

Roy: "I see where you're going: the Daribi modeling of their own ecological life-process, their *communality*, is not really *linear* at all, but center-peripheral, moving outward in all directions from a *dead center*."

Coyote: "Whereas the Aztecs, according to Miguel Leon-Portilla, called *their* version of the one-and-only God, *Moyucoyani* ('the God that *invented* himself'), the 'Lord of the Center and of the Periphery.' That betokens a wholly different form of interference-patterning, an *areal* or *circular* rendition of the Golden Section."

Roy: "Take a good look at figure 4, Coyote. It shows the difference between the linear and the circular renditions of the Golden Section in a very graphic way. Some very insightful archaeologists were searching among the ruins of the great Mayan city Palenque for any trace of a *standard unit of linear* measurement that could have been used by the ancient Mayans to lay out the foundations of their temples and other structures."

Coyote: "Let me guess: they couldn't find one."

Roy: "You got it. But then a local Mayan shoved them the secret of the *flower-petal*, or what might be called 'butterfly' diagrams. When the Mayans wanted to lay out the foundations of a building they would fix a centerpoint and incise a series of four, six,

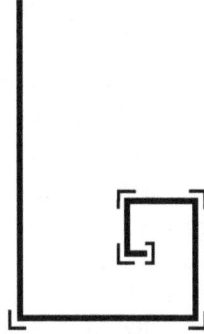

Graeco-Egyptian "labyrinth"

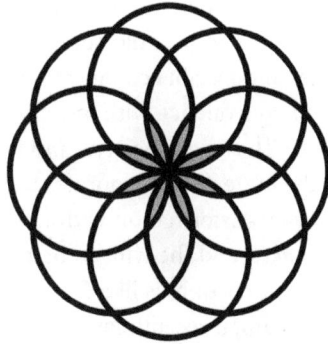

4. Circular, or Concentric Interference-Patterning

or eight circles in the ground, all of which met at that central
point and were all equal to one another, with their centerpoints
ranged around the periphery of that point."

Coyote: "Then the *interference-patterning* of the circles with one
another, as marked in figure 4, would be self-modeled within
the model of the diagram, and the whole effect of *dampening*
wave-trains, as in 'earthquake-proof,' as well as the *visual-
aesthetic* effect of the Golden Section, as in 'beauty,' 'the waters
of Lethe,' or 'the Parthenon,' would be realized in the construction of the Mayan edifice."

Coyote: "And so the 'butterfly' or 'flower petal' interference-patterning could be called the *picture-soul* of Mayan architecture."

Roy: "Because it is *drawn upon the earth*, one could say that the Earth Lord—the Mayan version of the *buruhoa*—taught it to them. And because the secret of the *butterfly* is that it incorporates the self-modeling of transformation within its own life cycle—egg larva chrysalis-winged being-egg—one could liken it to the design of the Mayan 'One and Only God,' the *Hunab Ku.*"

Coyote: "And because the Daribi self-generative process of communality is likewise *drawn upon the earth* (figs. 2 and 3) there is a strange *synchronicity* between the Daribi and the Mayan forms of *expersonation*. And because the *interference patterning* of circles ringing outward generates the spawning of Daribi intermarrying lineages as well as their sustenance and *manpower cascades*, one could conclude that the *picture-souls* of Mayan cities and Daribi ecological self-transformation show a remarkable co-equivalence with one another."

Roy: "The *birds*, the *bees*, and the *butterflies*, especially because the butterfly incorporates the Daribi mortality/immortality egg transformation within its own life-cycle. The larvae are like *snakes*, and the winged being is like a *bird*, whereas the chrysalis, or cocoon, is like Don Juan's luminous *egg*: the *picture-soul* of human recapitulation and self-imitative transformation."

Coyote: "Or at least trance-formation, eh, Roy? Like your *sonnets*, or like your personal fantasies about the monarch ('roy' meaning both 'red' and 'king'), the *totem bird* of those born in October."

Roy: "They all fly from different parts of the United States to a *single mountain* in Mexico, like, 'Tell him Groucho sent ya':

Monarchiad

Creation without hands, love without lies,
dark autumn knows the stars by undertow;
trees double-dye their foliage to show
deception as the map the monarch flies,

the tardy one, the next to last to know
the prostrate sun, the rivers cracking wise,
that thirty thousand gross of butterflies
take Santa Ana's road to Mexico,

So dense a boy could beat them with a stick,
and innocent of joy as sweet vermouth.
Vermillion is the *pro* that *turns the trick*,
it is no easy thing to tell the truth
and harder still to listen: flashbulb-quick
senescence imitates the surge of youth."

Coyote: "Tell 'em WALLACE STEVENS sent you!"
Roy: "So what is it we are modeling here? Is it the man who
    dreamt he was a butterfly, or a butterfly that dreamt it was a
    man?"
Coyote: "Roy, is it not you, yourself, who wrote the following, *and
    I quote*: 'The more suspect "language" itself becomes (in the un-
    dermining of credibility in its words and phrases, its concepts
    and ethnic background, its very authority), the greater the ten-
    dency to attribute weird, or highly inappropriate autonomies to
    the items of its inventory, invent "cultures," "symbolic construc-
    tions of reality," and even spiritual insights to explain them'"?

The Work of Language Is a Strange Device

Roy:

"And also the following:
No word is true until it mates in rhyme,
no language means itself apart from sound,
acoustically redundant, in the round;
the squares of grammar implicate a crime,
investigate the figure in its ground
until the sentenced culprit does its time.
There are no double meanings but sublime
cross-pollinating hybrids that redound

like poppy fields in breathing such a scent
that pheromonic colors take for rare,
that makes the RAINBOW think itself up twice.
The work of language is a strange device,
no recollection knows the way it went.
A symphony is made of empty air."

Coyote (quoting Wallace Stevens): "Let be be finale of seem / the only emperor is the emperor of ice cream."

Roy: "*Furthermore*, as I have *also* written, I can say a metaphor to you, regardless of whether I know what it means or not, and you assume I had known what I meant, and give me another metaphor to follow it, without you knowing the meaning of that metaphor either, and we could go at this play of assumptions all day *without either of us being the wiser.*"

Coyote: "I get your drift, Roy, and also your scent. See, your sonnets are too pat, too formal, too *finished*. They're not *icky* enough, not *wiggly* enough. Let me try my *paw*:

Diet of Worms
by Coyote

We sleep in sonnets, stigmatize the page,
somnambulate in corridors of dust
like annelidic psychos, held in trust
by anorectic shrinks of mucilage,
and con de scent of sources, come what must.
A book is Mother Nature's cryptophage,
the line a wormhole to some other age;
inscription is the ribbon-worm of lust.

For poetry is passion's parasite,
no telling where and when it lays its egg,
or why it lets the larvae out at night,
in what unholy corridors they kiss
and lie and steal, and sometimes even beg;
behold the language in its chrysalis."

Roy: "We have spoken a great deal about personal and cultural *clo-sure*—the *finishing* in any sense of the term, the *terminality*, the *terminix*." "

Coyote: "And last, but not least, the *termite*. We have digested a great deal about *worms*, and other icky and wiggly things, not to speak of *sonnets*."

Roy: "We have spoken a great deal about *representation, imper-sonation* and expersonation, self-modeling, the Mayans, the One and Only God, and the *merging with one's own reality* that makes closure of any kind, including death, anticlimactic and self-defeating."

Coyote: "But have we given any consideration to the fact that the *sonnet* has become, since the salad days of the Elizabethans, a sterile, antiquated, and monumental *relic*. And that, despite the triumphs of William Shakespeare, with his admittedly *chal-lenged* rhyme-schemes and juvenile addiction to *close-rhyming*: 'When in despite of worms, and fortune cookies / I seek my out-cast fate among the WOOKIES.'"

Roy: "The fate of an *impersonator*, you derivative canid. Content is everything, it's how you *say* it that counts. 'When, in despite of germs, and WOMEN'S eyes / and notwithstanding moths and butterflies / then every time I speak A COYOTE DIES.'"

Coyote (expires): "*Yechh.*"

Roy: "We only *pretend* to die, Coyote!"

Coyote (pretends to revive): "We only P R E T E N D to die?"

Roy: "Sure, the obvious facts of death are only a kind of 'cover,' a decoy for the *pragmatic afterlife*, the *real* expersonation that be-gan a long time before:

The Mirror Inside Out

Death has no other side, it's like a mirror
in which the shapes of life be multiplied,
an orbiture of color, double-dyed,
a hemisphere unto the hemis-fearer
adrenaline at heart, and mortified.

The signature of Lear upon the leerer,
like passion's second gear, but even queerer,
e-motion without *e.* Be satisfied.

To rhyme without a sound, to cite invective
without that Special One that makes it stick,
is harmful to the soul, and worse than wit—
reflection knows its own from counterfeit—
a mirror inside-out is not reflective,
so finish off this line, and make it quick.

Coyote: "So, in other words, the *medium of expression* through
which life represents itself to itself becomes the *expression of a
medium* that merges with its own reality, and appears as *death* to
everyone else."

Roy: "The *aristocratic way to emigrate*; a sonnet is the preferred
form of life-recapitulation—it gives you the *experience of facts*,
turns it around into *the fact of experience*, and then obviates
the image to show you the *real humor* of what was going on the
whole time. All sonnets are *funny*, Coyote, when you *get the
point*."

Coyote: "Still, it is hard to kill the suspicion that a sonnet is a purely *ornamental*, though admittedly lordly, archaeological ruin, or
rune. Like those amazing though utterly useless ROOF COMBS
that crown the Golden Section Mayan edifices to this very day."

Roy: "ROOF COMBS, Coyote? They *take the cake*:

Roof Combs

Too steep for architecture, stiff for arch,
they make the gods feel good for not existing
or acting up when stela-stones are listing.
At noon their self-important shadows march
like priests across the plaza. Not resisting
a single thing but gravity they parch
like corn in sunlight, give the rain its starch,
and flute the moon when valley floors are misting.

They comb the clouds, the wind and stars, and show
the world's impossibilities to law,
they do not go but upward, they command
attention in the heavens for the land.
'I MADE THEM THUS, MY NAME IS *YAX AHAW*,
THE LORD OF DISTANCE,' so the roof combs go.

Coyote: "So, *the fewer the gods, the better*, hey, like they *replaced*
their divinities with ROOF COMBS?"

Roy: "You just don't get it, do you? I mean, the *point* of divinity itself: *the better the fewer, the fewer the better*. Divinity is HOLO-
GRAPHIC, or it is *nothing*."

Coyote: "The odds are good, but the *goods* are odd."

Roy: "See, *Yax* (pronounced *yash*) is the color that archaeologists
call 'Mayan Blue,' the *background*, or *second attention* color that
Mayans used in their *power* depictions, much as the Byzantines
used a gold background in their *icons*. And blue is the *distance*."

Coyote: "But blue is the color that Goethe called 'an enchanted
nothingness' in his *Color-Theory*."

Roy: "Nonetheless, it is the Faustian color. And Mayans invented
the *zero*, didn't they."

HUNAB-KU; The WEAPONIZING of Anthropology

Coyote: "So what is the Hunab Ku?"

Roy: "It is the *terminator*, the *figure-ground* reversal of the zero,
the HORIZON of your lifetime, and anyone else's. It's what Don
Juan calls *the crack between the worlds*."

Coyote: "But it is only a simple *glyph*, a glyph depicting itself or
depicting itself depicting itself."

Roy: "Without attributes or characteristics, without *concrete* attributes or characteristics *power* would have no power, even
over itself. What was the first lesson that Don Juan taught
Castaneda?"

Coyote: "That peyote is not peyote but a powerful teacher and protector called *Mescalito*. That if you do not keep your *cool* un-

der the influence of an outside *agency*—hallucinogen or person—you will have a *bad trip*."

Roy: "Was it *superstition*, then, or some form of primitive *animism* that brought them to call the bomber that dropped the first atomic bomb the *Enola Gay*, and call the first atomic bombs 'Fat Man' and 'Little Boy?' Or call the first gigantic siege gun, back in the fourteenth century, *Mons Meg*, 'The Mountain, Margaret?' The Kaiser had 'Big Bertha,' and Admiral Nelson called his flagship the *Victory*."

Coyote: "The *object* must have part of the *person* or *user* in it, just as the user must incorporate the object within the leverage of their mind or body if they are to work in *tandem*, or mutual *confidence*. That is the secret of the *déjà vu* and the *vújà de*: what we call 'automation' is just simply a badass acknowledgment of this; a Coyote-copy."

Roy: "It's an old story, Coyote. That is why we give *names* to things, or write *sonnets* about them though they may be only vibrations of a fold in the throat. It *simply does not matter* whether the 'agency' is animate or inanimate, hallucinogenic or whatever. The way in which you treat the agency is the way the agency treats you: *whatever you put on it, it will put back on you*."

Coyote (quoting The Rolling Stones): "When you see her dressed in blue, like the sky in front of you . . . "

Roy: "SHE'S LIKE A R A I N B O W . . . "

Coyote: "HOW SWIFT THY DISPOSITION, HUNAB KU!"

Roy: "Like a work of classical music, *it grows in a dimension that is perpendicular to time* (Zuckerkandl). It is at one and the same time the center of the periphery and the periphery of the center. So now it's my turn,

Coyote: "What *is* the Hunab Ku?"

Coyote: "Well it *looks* (fig. 5) like a yin/yang figure *with balls*, or *wings*, like the Wrong Brothers' version of the Wright Brothers . . . THE HELICOPTER'S HALL OF FAME."

Roy: "Come on, now, BE SIRIUS, you dawg-star. What does it MEAN in terms of our discussion (or digression, as the case may be)?"

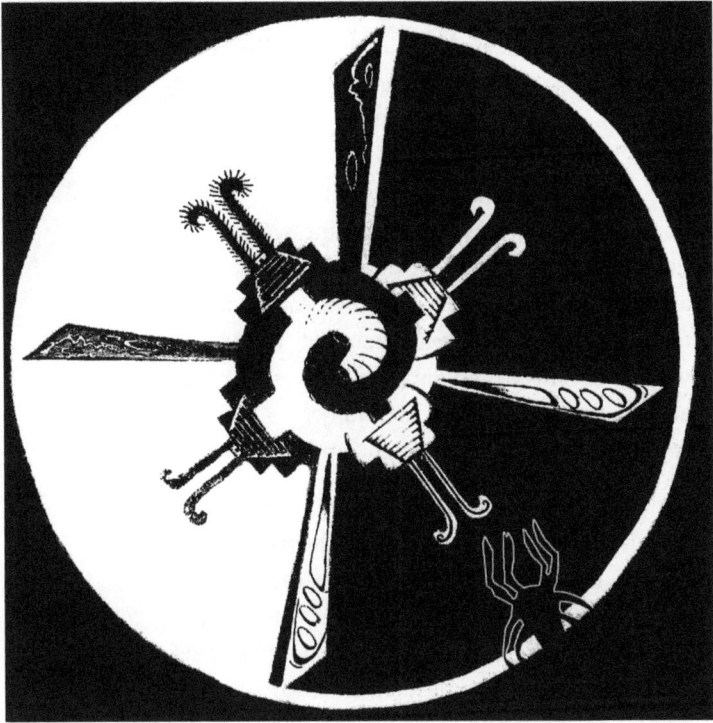

5. Hunab Ku: The One and Only God

Coyote: "A self-analytic re-programming of the reproductive life-
cycle, a mortality cum immortality trilogy that we found to be
generative of the Golden Section in the case of the Daribi."

Roy: "Far too abstract, Coyote. You're beginning to talk like an anthropologist. Remember what Don Juan taught about the *concrete* and *practical* essence of power. Remember that this is a
Mayan glyph, and, in fact, the glyph of all glyphs—a GOD."

Coyote: "Now *you're* beginning to talk like a Castanedan. In that
case it looks like one of those Mayan architectural 'flower petal' diagrams, complete with *stamens* and *pistils*. Or perhaps the
morning glory world of hummingbird, the Mayan Eclipse-Lord,
that sustains itself on the nectar of the flower: 'invisible, shot
through with eye and wing.'"

Roy: "That, too—Nature's helicopter, the terminator of the morning and evening twilight. The mutual transcendence, in life-cycle terms, of the night-living moth—Don Juan's 'Bearer of Knowledge'—and the day-living butterfly. Who feeds on jade and darkness?

The moon and Venus hang in solitude,
they whisper crickets, kindle darkness, brim
the deep cenote waters; world goes dim
and half-gods raise their eyebrows, eat the food
that turquoise lays beneath their feet. To him
who feeds on jade and darkness these are crude
and opalescent outlines; certitude
is measured on the fall of night, and slim.

The days are names that figures represent,
the nights are liquid voices, soon the bats
may eat the stars, and sleepers draw the breath
of daylight's syllabary through the spent
and shadowed worlds of dreaming on their mats;
the twilight is the gods' excuse for death.

Coyote: "So the TWINS of the *Popol Vuh*, the Mayan Book of Creation, are really, though I wouldn't believe it myself, A N T I-T W I N S."

Roy: "HOW SWIFT THY DEPOSITION, HUNAB KU! The *dark* worlds of the Mayans are ones that even *they* could not penetrate. They loved it that way."

Coyote: "They *made book* on it!"

Roy: "Hunab Ku is like the *recapitulation chamber* of the flower, bird, and insect world. You know, the ancient Meso-Americans had a totally different grasp of evolutionary cycles than we do. They claimed that each major order of creature had its turn at *sentience*: the insects, the birds, the lizards, the monkeys, and now the human beings."

Coyote: "I wouldn't bet on it; look how far I've gotten."

Roy: "Yeah, the HELICOPTER'S HALL OF FAME. No major civilization *makes it easy*. Those half-understood things we deign to comprehend as *civilizations* are there to PREVENT meaning, making it increasingly difficult either to deal with or *do something about*. Overspecialization, Tower of Babel stuff."

Coyote: "So the work, or *vocation*, of a 'civilization' is like your definition of humor: *getting the point by not getting it*? What we pretend, or at least *idealize* as the *truth* is not really the truth at all, but the OBVIATION of what happens when one gets caught in the *description*. *Any* description, of *anything*. OBVIATION lays bare the essential *humor* that lies behind any possible description, including the labyrinthine significance of the Hunab Ku."

Roy: "Oh, you NOTICED? If you are waiting for messages from *gods*, Coyote, you will have to wait a long time. They communicate largely in self-signs, postures and gestures, *innuendo*, raising their eyebrows, etc."

Coyote (scratching): "Well then we will have to start from scratch, like with what the Hunab Ku does *not* mean. The most obvious thing in the world is that the glyph represents the respective nocturnal and diurnal Lepidoptera, each evolving from the self-contained egg-larva-chrysalis-winged being lifecycle of the other. The day-moth and the night-butterfly. See the two opposite larvae, crawling out of the egg-like convolution at the center? As they grow and transform themselves into caterpillars, they eventually encapsulate themselves into chrysales, or cocoons—you can see their sensory antennae poking upward and out to the periphery. Whereas the bladelike diametrics, cutting the whole figure into four parts, are the *wings* of the beings that result, drying on the carapaces of their former cocoons and preparing for their nuptial flight out to the periphery."

Roy: "So if that is what it does *not* mean, then what it really means is the mutual OBVIATION of the moth by the butterfly, and the butterfly by the *moth*. Surrogates, of course, for the first attention and the second attention, or the tonal and the nagual, if you will."

Coyote: "The not-doing of a not-doing is simply another *doing*?
The picture of a fact is the fact of the picture?"

Roy: "Precisely. And it is impossible to picture a total transformation without transforming the *subject* as well; what you have
taken for *visual* is actually *acoustic*, what you have taken for larvae is actually the spinneret's of the SPIDER that ate 'em both,
and what you have taken for a cocoon is actually the crenulated
body of the spider."

Coyote: "And what I have taken for antennae are in fact the eight
legs of the spider, spread out to the four directions of the web.
And what I have taken for *wings* are the lethal blades of the web
itself, the center and periphery of a *killing machine*."

Roy: "The spider senses her prey through *vibrations* in the
tympanum:

To lick the wind with gossamer; insights
disguise a secret wounding of the lips,
there is no world beyond their fingertips,
no sky above their fickle northern lights.
Contained in syllabary craftsmanships
the tongue dissolves the senses' parasites;
the snare that caught the outer world requites
the webwork of the lungs in long ellipse.

The mind is like the DNA of sound
all spiraled into tone and iridescence;
a counterpoint of life, a killing zone
of echo-like vibrations in the round,
the melodies, the chords are of the essence,
and these in turn have spiders of their own.

Coyote: "SHOCK AND AWE; death by *chocolate*, death by *sex*,
death by something *too complex*. One thinks of the sacrificial
victims of the Aztecs and Mayans, of the world-creating spider
of the Oglala Sioux:

Transilient, its iridescence twinned
with something like to stardust out in space;
the widow-spider masks her person-face,
its RAINBOW-spittle gardening the wind,
with all the hanging trophies of the chase,
the dark fantastic mealtimes dried and spinned
"Like spinneret-kabobs," she winked and grinned,
"how many gave their lives to know this place?"

An agency's whatever does the works
when half-authentic beings have their say
like voices trapped within a symphony;
on every minor planet something lurks—
the minute *gods of dusk*, the lords of gray,
the spider-herding dreams of Sigma Three."

Spider: "I am your old Aunt Nancy, Anansi, Weaver of the Cloth
of Myth, come to tell you that you are both DEAD WRONG.
What is *unpictured* in the Hunab Ku is neither life nor death,
nor transformation, but the ultimate NOT DOING of all time:
the SOLAR ECLIPSE, the *coronal suture* of all thought and all
being. And it is the work of the ECLIPSE LORD, Hummingbird, the merciless WARRIOR GOD of scale change, and holography. Something SUBLIME, something akin to PURE LOVE:

No feather but a blur, and scarce the clearance
that folds the honeylove of butterfly;
old sunbeams turn to shadows when they die
and not for want of nuptial interference.
Mosaics worked in glass but cut the eye,
unglaze the RAINBOW in a brief appearance,
and have no mate nor meet for perseverance.
What wisdom contradicts the blossom's lie?

What jeweled shade decocts the atmosphere?
The deep end of the spectrum goes for this,
inebriate of darkness, half obscene

the wine of love. On anything but green
the bird that does not move, but just appear,
as angels do, and flowers, plants a kiss."

H. K.: "What? You mean I am not the *architectural masterpiece*
people have taken me for? That the so-called larvae or spin-
nerets are *not* the limestone conduit-channels of the cenotes,
curling beneath the Yucatec Mayan temples? That the so-called
cocoons or the spider's body are *not* foursquare Mayan temples,
facing upward to the *four directions*, with their ROOF COMBS
jutting upwards like *antennae*? That the so-called wings or killing blades of the web are *not* the resplendent glory-strokes of
feeding suffering to the gods?"

Hummingbird: "*No way*, Baby. Or, as Don Juan would put it, *nothing doing*. It goes back to the *self-eclipsing* of the human soul that
the Magistrate showed to Roy. *Lux et Tenebris*, don't you know,
like the SUNDIAL said: 'You are guided by *shadow*; I am guided
by *light*.' It goes to the SUBLIME NONEXISTENCE of the human soul. Perhaps John Donne would have said it the best. *Say
it like this*:

For concupiscence's sake, a great restrictor,
a soul is neither physical nor mental,
deliberate, or semi-accidental;
a different nothing negatives the victor,
the body and the mind, *experimental*,
for information is a poor predictor,
a lie unto itself, a truth-evictor,
and immortality is up for rental.

Some inadvertence, desperate and coy,
some greater sharpness whittles out the knife,
invisible and deft, and makes appliance
immune to purely abreactive science,
And such a prescience doth the soul enjoy:
it UNEXISTS to bring the rest to life.

Coyote: "So by now, Roy, we're all pissing RAINBOWS."

Roy: "Don't point!"

The Minute Gods of Dusk, the Lords of Gray

Coyote: "SEGUE. It is getting to be twilight at Karimui, the almost inaudible call of the *domuai* ('like an echidna'), a minute tree-frog, is sounding through the rainforest, a call so delicate and heart-wrenchingly beautiful that the Daribi reserve their designation solely for the naming of *very special* young girls, as the mark and measure of all impermissible delicacy on this earth."

Roy: "Roy is sitting in front of his tent, talking to Moses Hanari, son of the now-departed *RAINBOW-mastectomy* expert."

Coyote: "Moses is musing, as Daribi often do, on the peculiar characteristics of various forms of wildlife found in the area. He says, 'You know, cassowaries sometimes *bay like hounds*; I heard one once, and saw it coming down to the water.'"

Roy: "Then he says 'Listen, Roy; you can almost hear them, if you listen real close. That is the strange little snake that we call the *pini*, tiny, minute, they live *communally* in piles of debris on the forest floor. They go out in the twilight to search for food, and to communicate with one another they *whistle*.'"

Coyote: "So what? Lots of things live like that. Even coyotes do something like that, every once in a while."

Roy: "Not like *that*; he said they whistle on the IN-BREATH."

Coyote: "You mean like *taking all their words back* every time they speak? You mean that if they tried *mouth-to-mouth resuscitation* they would create a *meaning-vacuum* between them? It's like you said about *metaphor*, Roy: you and I could exchange *invisible meanings* all day long, and neither of us be the wiser."

Roy: "That would be *total obviation*. No, Coyote, as Groucho would say, 'close, but no cigar.' I was talking about the META-BREATH, the invisible but inseparable companion, the face-to-face ally that is with us every day of our lives and that departs at the moment of death."

Coyote: "You mean like, 'I met a breath, you meta breath, *every-body* gotta METABREATH?'"

Roy: "Closer yet, but no cigarette. The METABREATH is the one that breathes you in when you breathe out, and breathes you out again when you breathe in."

Coyote: "Wow! Tell me more about it."

Roy: "Don't hold your breath."

Three coyotes decided to take a train ride; they wanted to check out, well, maybe some sheep down the line. As they were buying their tickets they ran into three *live wires*, a.k.a. RAVENS, who were interested in currency and perhaps finding a nonconductor. The RAVENS bought only one ticket between them.

"Why did you guys buy only one ticket?" asked the coyotes.

"Watch and see," said the RAVENS.

When they all got on the train and it started moving, the three RAVENS all crowded into a john and closed the door. The coyotes took their seats and watched. When the conductor came around taking tickets he shouted into the john and said, "Tickets, please!" The door opened just a crack, and a beak poked out with a single ticket in it. The conductor took it and moved on. "Aha" said the coyotes, for they saw the RAVENS', trick (coyotes always say "Aha" in these stories, and RAVENS say "Oho"), "two of those bastards got to ride for free."

Well, there weren't no sheep on that there line, except maybe the coyotes themselves, so they got off at the next stop and decided to wait for the next train to go home again. The RAVENS got off, too, with the same idea in mind. *This* time, however ("Aha"), the coyotes bought only one ticket between them, but the RAVENS ("Oho") bought exactly *none*. "Why did you guys buy exactly no tickets?,"

"Watch and see" said the RAVENS, and they mumbled among themselves, quothing "NEVERMORE."

This time, when the train got underway, the three coyotes, who knew a thing or two, all jammed themselves into the john with their one ticket and closed the door. The three RAVENS who knew one thing more, found themselves another john, jammed in, and closed the door. After a little while one of the RAVENS snuck out of the door, hopped over to the Coyote's john, cleared his throat, and said, "AHEM, TICKETS PLEASE!"

Ever since that time coyotes have watched their back-track, ranchers have used electric fences, and passengers depend on nonconductors when they get their wires crossed. *Johns* are always jammed.

Negative Capability

Coyote: "So MEANING has been our big problem all along?"

Roy: "Ain't that the truth."

Coyote: "Well, *truth* too: it gets in the way of telling a better lie."

Roy: "Actually, NAMES are the real problem, as in 'the NAMED is the mother of the myriad creatures.'"

Coyote: "My mama was called 'Nomme du Chien.'"

Roy: "And that makes you a *very cross-breed*. A *hybrid*, like Bruno Latour says. You know, all the things we think, and all the things we do, which means especially *products*—they are neither *natural* nor *cultural*, but something in between—something *totally scary*. You would never want to look at it."

Coyote: "Like that Don Juan NOT DOING experiment you performed one summer evening with the huge white oak tree, while sitting on your deck. Remember?"

Roy: "Don Juan told Carlos to study the shadows of a tree, isolate the darkness within it and around it as if it were a separate, freestanding thing in itself—*Ding an Sich*. But the tree was so huge, over there on the ravine, that I could only *do* it part by part. I studied and grouped one part of the tree's darkness after another, carefully *convincing my body* that the shadows were real and the visible tree-outline was not."

Coyote: "But it was getting dark—you know, TWILIGHT and all—so you *gave up*, didn't you. You got up from the chair and turned around to go into the house."

Roy: "The *visual memory* is a very strange thing, Coyote—it collects the whole even when you're not aware of it."

Coyote: "Sure, Roy, and the *soul* is even trickier—it UNEXISTS to bring the rest to life. And you made the mistake of *looking back*. NEVER LOOK BACK."

Roy: "And what I saw there, standing where the oak tree should have been, was a M O N S T R O S I T Y that will haunt me all the days of my life."

Coyote: "Time's movie of itself, the NEGATIVE NEGATIVE. Like that other oak tree showed you, the one in the cemetery at Lexington, Virginia, by Stonewall Jackson's grave."

Roy: "It was a giant among giants, and what it said—like projecting word-images in my mind—was, 'YES, I WAS HERE BEFORE THE CITY OF LEXINGTON WAS HERE, AND I WAS HERE BEFORE THE WHITE MAN WAS HERE, AND ALL THE TIME BETWEEN THEN AND NOW IS LIKE A SINGLE I N S T A N T.'"

Coyote: "So did the tree OBVIATE you, or did you OBVIATE the tree?

Roy: "Obviously, there is no such thing as OBVIATION, Coyote."

Coyote: "That is what makes it so POWERFUL."

Getting a Grip on OBVIATION

Roy: "You gotta *control* yourself, Coyote. You gotta *grasp that amoeba firmly by the pseudopod*."

Coyote: "You gotta get a *grip* on yourself, Roy. You gotta chop that *negative negative* tree down and use it for firewood."

Roy: "So, *in other words*, we gotta PRETEND that OBVIATION is possible even though we know for a *fact* that it does not exist."

Coyote: "We gotta find a SUBSTITUTE for OBVIATION, given that SUBSTITUTION is the very essence of what we are talking about."

Roy: "And *how*. It is the only thing that ever goes on in conversation or myth—it's the dialectic. And all we ever get of language is the *myth* of language. For without the *concrete* embodiment of what language is talking about—the myth of the image in the image of the myth—language itself would lack for concrete dimensions."

Coyote: "Nobody ever learned *anything* from pure abstraction."

Roy: "Shucks, even *pure abstraction* never learned anything from pare abstraction."

Coyote: "Language invents image and then image invents the language."

Roy: "The OBVIATION DIAGRAM invents the OBVIATION DIAGRAM (fig. 6) and then the OBVIATION DIAGRAM invents the myth."

Coyote: "I thought the myth was the first thing the human race ever knew."

Roy: "Nope, it's the *second thing*: narrative sequency. SUBSTITUTION was the first thing the human race ever knew. You know, the best SUBSTITUTE for a SUBSTITUTE is a SUBSTITUTE. Like what I once called 'The Most Original Joke of All.'"

Coyote: "Then the *third thing* is the SYNTHESIS, the point of *closure* in a myth—the *punch line* of a joke. Like, you know, the great invention of Hegel: *the Buck stops here.*"

Roy: "Hegel never made any *doe.*"

Coyote: "That is because he forgot about FIGURE-GROUND REVERSAL, the synthesis INVERTED upon itself. You don't *figure*, you don't *ground*. You must have had a pretty *abstract* sex life back there in Jena."

Roy: "G. W. F. Hegel imagined that his discovery of the *synthesis*, or closure of the dialectic, bespoke the end of history. But what it really did was take him back to the *beginning* of human thought: *grounding the figure by figuring the ground. Joke*, see? '*In Jena geht es wunderlich / Dass weisst die Ganze Welt.*' What *we* gotta do is bring his magnificent discovery *up to speed*, relocate it on the timeline."

Coyote: "*Precisely*. And we can do that best by introducing the ANTI-SYNTHESIS, the *figure-ground reversal* of the synthetic triangle, and which proceeds by acts of CANCELLATION *disguised* as SUBSTITUTIONS."

Roy: "'It is at *twilight*,' said Hegel, 'that the Owl of Minerva spreads

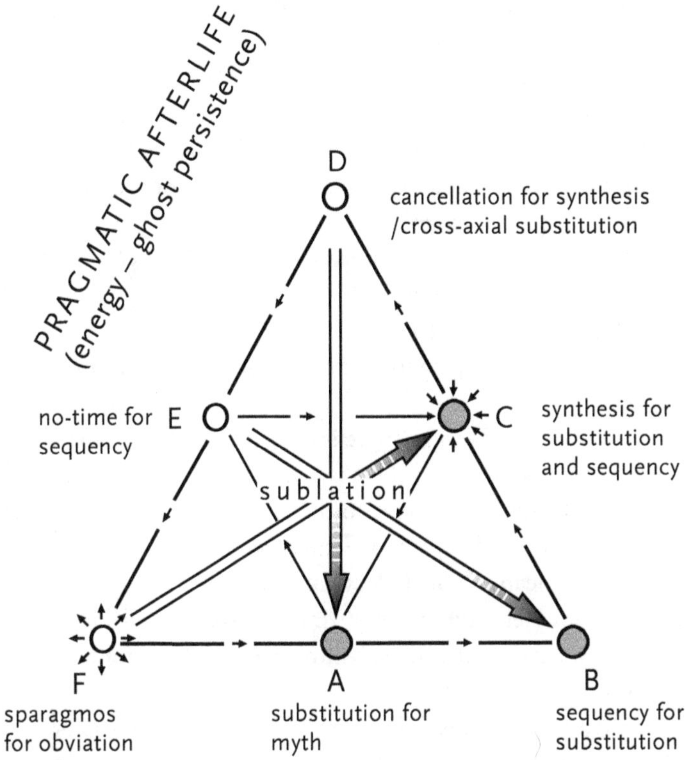

The Obviation Diagram labels:

PRAGMATIC AFTERLIFE (energy – ghost persistence)

D — cancellation for synthesis /cross-axial substitution

no-time for sequency E

C — synthesis for substitution and sequency

sublation

F — sparagmos for obviation

A — substitution for myth

B — sequency for substitution

6. The Obviation Diagram

her wings.' And that means *pragmatic afterlife*, energy-ghost persistence, the *down-stroke*; what the old drama-theorists called the *denouement*, the 'falling action.'"

Coyote: "So the best way to understand the DIAGRAM (fig. 6) is to make it *self-analytic* in its own terms, make it *draw a picture of itself*. Else it would only be a *myth-understanding*, like what happened to Hamlet back at Elsinore."

Roy: "Substituting his MAD self for his other MAD self."

Coyote: "So how does it work?"

Roy: "It doesn't, that's the point."

Coyote: "So let's start at A, the very *bottom*, where the *concrete* mostly gets you."

Roy: "We substitute the *act* of substitution for the myth itself, substituting in the myth one person, thing, episode, or concept for another establishes the *basis* for OBVIATION."

Coyote: "And then go on to B, *sequency for substitution*: the *narrative sequency* or temporal continuity of the story is substituted for the principle of substitution itself. From now on it's *one damn thing after another*."

Roy: "But HARK, can it be? It must be, I hear *hunting horns*, it *sounds* like our old friend . . . "

Hegel: "Da ist wieder der Hirsch . . . "

Coyote: "What is he trying to say? Quick, Roy, I need a *translation, fast*."

Roy: "Not so fast. After all, 'There is once again the stag; the learned philosopher from Jena is trying to tell what has got to be the oldest German joke on record: "There is once again the stag at which your Lordship every winter shoots."'"

Coyote: "You mean the Buck *does not* stop here?"

Roy: "Only for Hegel did it every winter do so. You tell a joke / *it* tells on you. At point C we substitute SYNTHESIS for both substitution and sequency."

Coyote: "And that means *full closure* for the initial *scenario* of the story or joke—where the Buck *trips up*. From then on the OBVIATION goes into *figure-ground reversal, energy-ghost persistence*."

W.S.: "Now bid the stricken deer go weep, the hart ungalled play / for some must watch while others sleep, so runs the world away."

Roy: "You see, D is the *midpoint* of the OBVIATION, the place where *figure-ground reversal* kicks in. *Cancellation* SUBSTITUTES itself for the merely *synthetic* closure, and does so on the *downstroke*, the first *cross-axial* substitution, *taking out* A, so all we have left is B, C, and cancellation itself."

Coyote: "We have nothing left to SUBSTITUTE for SUBSTITUTION."

Roy: "And, as you may have noticed, SUBSTITUTION is *nothing less* than the very principle of *synchronicity*, or *co-incidence*. And it *just so happens* that, synchronicity being the very *presence* of time, we have NO TIME left."

Coyote: "So there is only one thing left to do: SUBSTITUTE *NO TIME* for the *presence* of time itself, at E, cancelling out *sequency* at B, and leaving us with only C, D, and E."

Roy: "Which is hardly a coincidence, because at this point there is nothing left to follow and all we can do is *fall.* 'Here falling suits us best,' as Rilke said in "An Hölderlin," his magnificent apostrophe to the poet Hölderlin:

Oh you wandering spirit, the most restless of all. How they
live snug in their overheated verses, lingering long
in the small comparison, taking part. But you only
drift, ghosting like the moon. And below brightens and darkens
your holy terrified landscape
that you know only in farewells . . . "

Coyote: "So point F, cancelling point C on the *backstroke*, is the total inside-out *inversion* of what a SYNTHESIS would have to be; what the ancient Greeks call the *sparagmos*, the 'scattering.' The SUBSTITUTION of pure abandon, or detachment, for the whole set of operations that have guided us around the so-called hermeneutical circle. Tell me, Roy: is that what you call OBVIATION?"

Roy: "Not unless you are willing to 'linger longer in the small comparison.' OBVIATION is a *fractal*, or scale-retentive feature, that is evident (made *obvious*) at every point, and the 'circle' is not a circle at all, but a *triangle.*"

Coyote: "So the real stroke of OBVIATION would be the *contrast*, the humor or irony brought into stark realization between the *sparagmos* at F and the original SUBSTITUTION at A, that set the whole myth in motion in the first place."

Roy: "Right on, Coyote. And because that 'humor' or 'irony,' as you call it, *goes beyond all understanding* and is in fact exactly the sort of MONSTROSITY that ruined my whole day when I did Don Juan's NOT-DOING exercise with the tree-visualization, it *is impossible to put into words, or even thoughts.* It is what Hegel called the SUBLATION."

Coyote: "Then you will just have to *walk me through it.* Like, What really happened to Hamlet? Not the Hamlet in Shakespeare's magnificent dramatic elucidation but the NOT-DOING Hamlet, the tree-visualization Hamlet? You know, like that ancient Kabbalistic notion of *the tree that grows inward to its own seed*."

Roy (somewhat exhausted): "Go back to figure 6 and follow me, step by step. A: Prince Hamlet, faced by seemingly incontrovertible evidence that his uncle Claudius had *m*urdered his father, took the decision to *act himself mad* so he could speak the truth and disqualify that truth even as he spoke it. He could then say what no Crown Prince was ever allowed to say, and so OBVIATE the purpose of the new King Claudius."

Coyote: "But then B (SUBSTITUTING sequence for substitution), he encounters the court adviser Polonius, father of his staunch friend Laertes, and of his intended fiancée, Ophelia. Polonius is famous for his almost-wise saying, 'To thine own self be true,' counseling *the exact opposite* of the course that Hamlet elected to follow."

Roy: "And it is the unspeakable *irony* caught between those two very different *courses of action* that accounts for what happens in the SYNTHESIS, point C (SUBSTITUTING the SYNTHESIS for both *sequency* and substi*tution*). Hamlet decides to spring his trap. He gets some traveling players to perform a *dumb show*, the famous 'play within a play,' before the whole court. The play is supposed to show a man murdering his own brother by pouring poison into his ear, and so OBVIATE the crime of Claudius, by making it *obvious* to everyone without words."

Coyote: "But what the dumb show *does in fact show* is not that at all, but *a nephew murdering his own uncle*. This *tips the hand* of the requital that Hamlet was plotting, or, in other words, OBVIATES Hamlet himself, instead of Claudius."

Roy: "From that point onward the action goes into reverse mode, *figure-ground reversal, cancellation, and falling action*; pragmatic afterlife, as it were. The hero is now running in a *relative trajectory* and cannot act for himself anymore. Here is where the Buck *starts*."

Coyote: "D: CANCELLATION for SYNTHESIS, cross-axial SUBSTITUTION. Hamlet goes to confront his mother in her room and is *startled* by a movement behind the arras (tapestry). Thinking it to be Claudius, already wise and spying on them, Hamlet *runs him through with his rapier*. But, alas, 'I took thee for thy better,' it is NOT Claudius but that dim-witted expert on truth-detection, *Polonius*. This effectively CANCELS (D-A) the *mad for sane* SUBSTITUTION with which the whole charade had begun."

Roy: "In *no time flat* Hamlet has just done to Laertes (*and* Ophelia) *just exactly* what Claudius had done to *him*: he *murdered their father*. E effectively *cancels out* the counsel of Polonius, which came *in sequence* after Hamlet's original strategy-decision. Now the betrayed Laertes is exactly *on a par* with Hamlet, except of course Hamlet himself is the betrayer. Hence the bizarre significance of E: Claudius, now wiser than ever, loses *no time* in conspiring with Laertes to set up a *duel to the death* disguised as swordplay, before the whole Elsinore court."

Coyote: "And what you called the *sparagmos* just naturally fell into place. Through their respective machinations—poison, swordplay, etc.—practically everybody dies except Horatio. And all as a result of the self-betraying *dumbshow*, at the point of SYNTHESIS, at C. F CANCELS out that SYNTHESIS (F-C *on the backstroke*), bringing its ominous forebodings *full circle*."

Roy: "But it was LAERTES, it could only have been Laertes, who *saw* the whole play of *circumstance* behind the whole dumb show: HE SAW THE TREE! As he lay dying on the boards he screamed at Hamlet: KILL THE KING! And so Hamlet, as his last desperate act on this earth, goes and does so."

Coyote: "So the real HERO of *Hamlet, The Obvious*, is actually Laertes!"

Roy: "*No way*, Coyote. The Tiv people of Nigeria called *him* a *witch*! Obviation is *never what you think it is*, and there was another more powerful drama going on behind our backs this whole time. And it is the play of:

Fortinbras, the Not-So-Mad Berserker from Norway

Coyote: "So the TREE of NOT-DOING never looks the same way twice?"

Roy: "Hell, Coyote, it never even looks the same way *once—you* have to do the looking."

Coyote: "You gotta *watch* those *Vikings*; just turn your back and they'll discover America."

Roy: "And call it Vinland, the Good. (!) The SUBSTITUTION through which the drama began was that of Hamlet's missed successorship to the throne of Denmark. Fortinbras (Norman for 'Strong Arm') took advantage of the 'scattering' (F), F-C, obviating the original SYNTHESIS, to SUBSTITUTE his own power for the series of failed SUBSTITUTIONS A-F."

Coyote: "Only because of the 'empty time' at E, and the *falling out* of the principals precedent to Hamlet's and Laertes' dual. (F-E; *reverse temporal motivation*)."

Roy: "But that was only because of Hamlet's *mistake* in skewering Laertes's dad, Polonius, instead of Claudius, behind the arras at D, CANCELING the original SUBSTITUTION at A. Itself a natural consequence of the failed SYNTHESIS at C, wherein the 'play within a play' tipped the hand of Hamlet's revenge (E-D-C; *reverse temporal motivation*). That was Fortinbras's secret: the plot, and virtually every OBVIATION, is psychologically *motivated backward*, giving the protagonists a kind of precognitive view of what will happen—a sort of 'future memory,' or *future-in-its-own-past*."

Coyote: "So let me get this straight: the death of Claudius *motivated* the duel, which in turn motivated Laertes to act in collusion with Claudius *because* Hamlet had taken out his illocutionary opposite at D. And that, in turn, happened precisely because the dumb show SYNTHESIS, at C, showed the opposite of what it was supposed to show, consequent upon Polonius's 'wise words' at B, which naturally came about because of Hamlet's decision to act himself mad at A. Just who is this Fortinbras guy, anyway? Did he actually *live time backward*, like the wizard Merlin in King Arthur's court?"

Roy: "No, he was only doing what any straight-thinking Norse leader would do,: act *berserk*, instead of merely mad. And besides, this is only a myth, and a myth is always transparent to itself. Just like real life, as it were."

Coyote: "And behind that prima facie evidence—the Plot—lies another *subplot*, eh? Like the one that moved Fortinbras in what you humans would like to call Shakespeare's *subconscious*. Lay it on, Roy, lay it on *real thick*."

Roy: "No need to get bent out of shape. Backward, forward, what's the difference? There is much good evidence that people are in fact motivated by real or anticipated future events, that we *remember the future* at least as well as we remember the past. But we have a great fear, or hesitation, about *admitting that fact to ourselves*. It *terrifies* people, Coyote, like the *tree*, and forces them to tell myths instead, like 'mostly harmless' surrogates."

Coyote: "So what is *really* going on in OBVIATION?"

Roy: "I'd *tell* ya, but then I'd have to *show* ya, which I will in fact do, in figure 8. But first, see, a metaphor or trope is not what it seems to be. It is the *thin edge of the wedge* of something much larger, something that is *totally encompassing*."

Coyote: "Like a joke or a pun *disqualifies itself*, keeps the possibility of an *all-encompassing* humor from getting out and disintegrating the world of commonplace, respectable *seriousness*. That is why people *pretend* to hate puns—they destroy language's ability to *picture*, which is the *legal basis* of, among other things, morality."

Roy: "The *figure-ground reversal*, as in *Hamlet, The Obvious*, and *Fortinbras, The Unobvious*, is the SECOND POWER, or what mathematicians could call the POWER SET of the world of metaphors. *All* the metaphors; not only jokes and puns but all the secular, religious, artistic, and scientific metaphors that make up the *whole library* of our ability to *picture facts to ourselves."*

Coyote: "So now don't tell me, Roy, let me guess: there is a THIRD POWER that controls the world and action of figure-ground reversals just as surely as figure-ground reversal itself controls our ability to intuit, to imagine, to remember, to *conceive mentally*. And that THIRD POWER is OBVIATION."

Roy: "Not so fast, Coyote. It is the end-result of OBVIATION, the sublime *motivator* of the whole obviative process. It is what Hegel called SUBLATION: *underdetermining the sides, sub-latio*, just as *re-latio* means 'relation,' putting the sides together."

Coyote: "Then *sublation* would be the opposite of *both* sparagmos and SYNTHESIS. THIS, I gotta see!"

Roy: "You'll *see* it in a minute, and it goes like this: if a myth, tale, or legend, or an *explanation* (which is the same thing) is a verbal picture of itself, or an *image* told in many episodes—each substituted for the previous—then it must have a point of OBVIATION. A *vanishing point* where all its episodes and pictographic details merge together to form a single holographic entity, the tiniest part of which is equal to the whole."

Coyote: "Don Juan calls this the 'abstract core' of the story, the part that cannot be verbalized no matter how many times you repeat it. By contrast, of course, *I* am just a concrete *flake*."

Roy: "Save your *archaeology* for Indiana Jones. To illustrate why this must be so and what OBVIATION means ('to anticipate and dispose of'), perform a simple experiment: Using a light source, project the image of a triangle, the simplest linear figure, through an inverting lens and onto a screen, as with a slide projector. Now the 'image' itself, the triangle, is *exactly the same* (e.g., isomorphic) throughout the sequence, though it shows as right-side-up and upside-down at opposite ends of the continuum. But at the *focal point* of the lens—which 'twists' the image through 180 degrees—the isomorphic image exists as a dimensionless point."

Coyote: "That is the vanishing point of knowledge and the emer-

gence of *silent* knowledge that the MYTHOLOGY of OBVI-
ATION seeks to establish? *Now* I *see* it."

Roy: "Now I don't. The Creator need not have created the world
after all, but only the MYTH of the world's creation. In short,
there *is* no universe of *extensions* (e.g., space or time) but that
there must be, at some point in its continuum, a nondimension-
al abstract core, an UNEXTENDED image, that is isomorphic
with all reality. That point is both the *origin* and the *demise* of all
the stories or explanations that could be told of it."

Coyote: " What Hamlet and Laertes or Hamlet and Fortinbras
knew but *could not tell each other* . . . "

Roy: " . . . or even themselves . . . "

Coyote: " . . . *each being the result of false claims made upon the
other*, that the world as they knew it *goes all the way through* that
point of NONEXTENSION and comes out the other side."

Roy: "They were like players in a chess game, each playing the *inside* of the other's strategy."

Coyote: "But from a *parallactic* viewpoint there was only one strategy after all, the one that the GAME itself knows."

Roy: "Goes to Wagner's Law: 'Of all the possible things that could
happen in the next moment, *only one of them will*.'"

Coyote: "Goes to *Shakespeare's* insight: *There Are More Things in
Heaven and Earth, Horatio, than Are Dreamt in Your* . . . "

Roy: "*OBVIATION*. What is actually OBVIATED in a myth is the
self-sustaining structure of three-dimensional reality—the kind
of mathematical approximation in which 'dimension' becomes
a viable means of describing space through the dependency of
each particular 'dimension' upon the other two (add more if you
want to *really* screw yourself up)."

Coyote: "In this sense people would *have* myths, or try to know
the world of experience through them in order to OBVIATE the
kinds of problems that spatial extension poses for them."

Roy: "Figure 7, created from the self-inversion of Penrose's 'impossible' tribar, makes use of the OBVIATION diagram itself to
dramatize the 'dimensional' perplex of the OBVIATION pro-

cess. In this case the *holographic* aspect of OBVIATION is very hard to miss . . . "

Coyote: " . . . or *comprehend*, either . . . "

Roy: "That, too. Look at figure 7; each of the lettered (A, B, C) SUBSTITUTIONS is situated at a point of paradox vis-à-vis the other two points on its particular triangle, and each is at the opposite-but-coordinate point (the NOT-NOT) of the SUBSTITUTION that is opposite to it within the whole (e.g., two triangles) figure."

Coyote: "This means that the two triangles that form the figure itself

stand in a relation of complete cancellation to one another, as well as to themselves. Each OBVIATES itself, and also the positioning of the other. Thus, since each triangle by itself comprises and exhibits the effect of three-dimensional OBVIATION, and does so by virtue of the other, a totally HOLOGRAPHIC set of procedural possibilities is set up. This means that *any* three SUBSTITUTIONAL points on the whole figure can be used to form an OBVIATIONAL triangle in opposition to any three others."

Roy: "It means much more than that, Coyote. It means that each SUBSTITUTION creates and manifests a whole world unto itself, that each could act fully on a *par* with the others. Every particular SUBSTITUTION within an OBVIATION is, from its own perspective, an *axis* upon which the whole thing turns. You could begin the myth at any point, provided you come *full paradox* around the diagram, and complete it with a SUBLATION at that point."

Coyote: "So back to the story of Hamlet. Beginning and ending at point B we have the *equally probable* drama entitled: 'Polonius; Wise Soothsayer of Elsinore, And How He Got His Errant Son-in-Law to Prove His Words True.' Beginning and ending at point C: 'The Smart Dumb-Show Players, And How They Tricked a *Real* Nephew into Murdering His False Uncle.' Beginning and ending at D: 'It's *Curtains* for You; How a Simple Tapestry Brought Down Two Adults with a Single Blow.'

Roy: "Notwithstanding the main point, A-SUBLATION: 'And

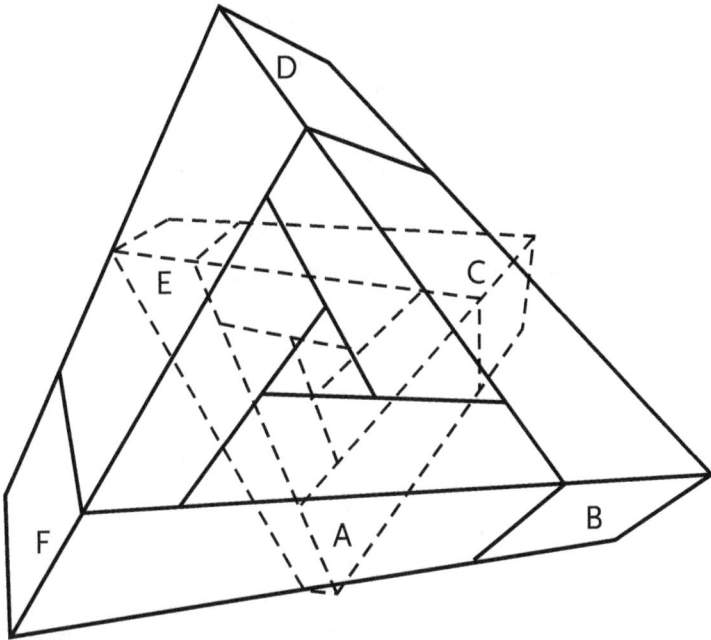

7. Pragmatic Afterlife Re-Envisioned: What Laertes Saw in Hamlet

Flights of *ANGLES*. Sing Thee to Thy Rest.' Laertes *saw it all in a flash*; both *past-ness* and *futurity* are actually *consumed* by the effort to *get past it*. Laertes *did not see* that both Hamlet and Fortinbras were *living each other's obviation backward*, he only saw a *way out*. Fortinbras saw a way *in*. Laertes saw a PARADOX."

Coyote: "*Doctor* Hamlet, Esq., from Wittenberg, and *Doctor* Fortinbras, Inq. from the School of Hard *Knox*."

Roy: "And also, alas, Doctor FAUSTUS, Relativity Incarnate, the secret motivator of the whole Reformation period upon which Shakespeare himself had *cut his teeth*. The Creator, Coyote, had no need to create the physical, material universe, but only create the MYTH of the world's creation."

Coyote: " Once that myth was OBVIATED, come full circle, He was *already there* at the Beginning. Point A prime: Alpha et Omega. 'The Story of a Simple SUPREME BEING, And How He Got the UNIVERSE to Do His Work for Him.'"

Roy: "What we have here, Coyote, in the guise of a Supreme Being, is SUBLATION, the Buck that Never Stops, the sublime *motivation*, or HOLOGRAPHIC movement, of the whole creation. It is the AUTOMIMETIC AGE, ROY that imitates you, *models* you, if you will, far better than you could ever imitate or *model* it."

Coyote: "So Spengler should have called this the HAMLET Culture instead of the FAUSTIAN Culture, though there is that little thing about selling one's soul to the devil for power, or at least *profit*."

Roy: "Prince Hamlet did something far worse: he sold his soul to AUTOMIMETIC AGENCY."

Coyote: "And Prince Fortinbras bought it, lock, stock, and barrel."

Roy: "He bought it in what might be called the SUBLATIVE tense, or mode, a kind of exponential realization of the *subjunctive*, or 'as if,' and is intimately related to the agentive confusion between past-in-its-own-future and future-in-its-own-past."

Coyote: "Like *pragmatic afterlife*, 'energy-ghost persistence' is the place where the AUTOMIMETIC AGENCY of the myth takes over from the storyteller? Like the Last Judgment is the *youngest* judgment of all?"

Roy: "Like Paul Riceour's famous *observation* that 'the meaning of a myth does not lie behind it, but *in front of it*.' And especially like that age-old mistake that astronomers make about the so-called fossil, light that reaches us from distant objects out in interstellar space, and gives us all the information we will ever know about the universe."

Coyote: "We have no evidence at all that the light is not its own AUTOMIMETIC AGENCY, stealing its own message, as it were."

Roy: "But we have *plenty* of evidence that it *is*, such as Einstein's famous equation $E = mc^2$. If the velocity of light is a *constant*, as Einstein showed is the case, then *everything else* is its AUTOMIMETIC variable. For by *transposition*, c, the velocity of light, *is equal to the square root* of energy divided by mass and, *as in any other quadratic equation, the flux of universal transformation* can take either positive or negative values. It *copies* the way that the universe behaves *better* than the universe can copy *it*; it steals its own message."

Coyote: "So light *in and of itself* is the *meaning* and the *myth* of the universe, the *subliminal* of the *subluminal,* as it were. As you once put it, Roy, '*Light artificially ages the cosmic expanses around it as it pretends to move through them, growing FOR-EVER YOUNGER as it travels; it gives us a totally dissimulative picture of the motion and composition of the universe.*' (Take that, Caltech!) Light is the ultimate *gravity lens* (see fig. 7)."

Roy: "In this case *seeing* is not quite the same thing as believing—in fact, it is the very opposite. *I could show thee infinity in a nutshell.*"

Coyote: "And I thee in a *nutcase.* You have shed absolutely *no light* on the subject, and as you yourself have put it [chap. 1]: 'The job of stars is *staying up all night* / to intimate insouciance to the mind.'"

Roy: "And as I myself have written, in my not-so-very-famous afterword to *On the Order of Chaos*:

What medium of representation shall we use to represent that which represents itself better than we can represent it, that automimetic quality that Richard Dawkins has called the 'meme' (The cat family seems to have evolved by 'stalking'—imitating its own nonpresence to its prey, so I have used it here as a totem for the automimetic; Hamlet ('To be or not to be') is the automimetic hero of our literature. Wittgenstein ('We picture facts to ourselves') was the philosopher of the meme). Language itself acquires a self-similarity when it mimes the things of which it speaks, and because that self-similarity is both tighter than logic and looser than fiction, much of my prose seems to be about itself in a sort of free-associational wordplay."

Coyote: "Cheer up, Roy. You've made it Big Time—you're way up there with Erving Goffman, you know, 'Secretly controlling the one who thinks they've been controlling you all along, and then allowing *them* to imagine that *they* have been doing the same thing to *you,* but only as COVER for the fact that it was really *two different people* all along and we, ourselves, none the wiser . . . "

Roy: "Nor even *they,* like *ships passing . . .* CHIPS *parsing . . .* CHAPS POSING . . . "

Coyote: "KNIGHTS, Roy, KNIGHTS, like KNIGHTS PISS-ING IN THE SHAFT. Dammit, can't even get a simple cliché straight. What this whole thing reminds me of is the *voice* of the meme, similar to how the science fiction authors used to talk about The *VOICE.*"

VOICE of the Meme

Roy: "Reminds *me* of the Daribi tale of *Pozhubo, po wabo,* "he ut-ters," being (scant wonder) an *irregular* verb in that language. The infix *zhu* here indicates 'exclusive,' so his name means 'He (exclusive) speaks.'"

Coyote: "The fully autonomous, no-holds-barred *one liner.*"

Roy: "*Tell* me about it:

Some children were going along the Tua River. They came across a pandanus tree growing by the water, took some fruit from it, and returned home. When they broke open the fruit pod to pre-pare it for cooking, they found a man inside, who leapt out and ran into a drum, carrying a miniature bow and arrows with him. All of the men came together, and one decided to look into the drum. When he did so, the little man shot him in the eye with an arrow, and he died. Then another man got up and looked into the drum, and he was shot in the eye and killed also. This went on until all the men in the line were killed except one. He didn't know about the little man in the drum. He slept and had a dream in which his brothers came and said, 'We were all killed by a little man who is inside the drum; he shot us each in the eye.' In the morning the man arose and went to find a *sogoyezi-bidi* (shaman). The *sogoyezibidi* came up to the house, and the man told his wife to kill a pig. After they had cooked and eaten the pig the *sogoyezibidi* smoked some tobacco and then told the man that his brothers had indeed been killed by a man in the drum when they had looked inside. Then the man fastened a stone to the top of the drum and another to the bottom and carried it outside. The man said, 'I'll let him out here.' The little man in the drum, however, said, 'You may not let me out here or in your garden; carry me to another place and release me.' They came to another place, and the man said he would let the little man out there, but he replied, 'No, you hunt here and make your gardens here.' They came to the mountain Dogu, and again the man wanted to release him, but he said, 'No, keep carrying me.' Finally they came to the two mountains called Kegena and Samanawe, and the man opened the drum and looked inside. But the little man had already gone to the mountain, and shouted back, 'I've gone already.' Then the little man shouted down that the man should cut off all his hair. When he had done this he called back, and the little man told him to take his clothes off. He said, 'I have taken them off.' 'Alright, now cut your earlobes.' 'Done.' 'Now cut your nasal septum.' 'Done.' 'Now cut your penis.' The man went to cut his penis, but now he fell dead. The little man up on the mountain said, 'Oho, oho.' People used to see his campfire up on the mountain, but now he has gone. His name was Pozhubo."

Coyote: "So the *difference* between the visual and the acoustical is the *meme*."

Roy: "Now cut your tail, Coyote."

Coyote: "And the difference between the VOICE and the CHOICE is the *command*."

Roy: "Now cut your *talk*."

Coyote (gagging): "So where did the *command decision* come from?"

Roy: "It's where it *went* that counts."

Coyote: "And where did it *go*?"

Roy: "It OBVIATED, it *recapitulated* all the indignities suffered upon the person of its hapless victim."

Coyote: "The tale begins with an anomaly, a miniature human being replete with bow and arrows, discovered within a pandanus pod (SUBSTITUTION A: miniature person for pandanus pod). Freed of its integument, the imago rushes into the likewise tubular body of the characteristic hourglass-shaped drum. It exchanges one sort of tubular integument for another, but it is significant in that the drum is a sound-producing communicative device (SUBSTITUTION B: drum for imago, sound-producing integument for silent edible one). As the men peer into the drum, one by one, to try and discern the shape of their visitor, they are visually fixated, shot, and killed. The attempt to foil the visitor by recourse to visual communication is turned to the visitor's advantage; the men render themselves vulnerable by exposing their eyes (SYNTHESIS C: eye-death for attempted communication)."

Roy: "The surviving man realizes that a different sort of 'seeing,' that of the shaman, is in order, and, accordingly, he brings one, who is able to divine the identity of the visitor and confirm the purport of the man's dream (CANCELLATION D: begin *Falling Action*: spiritual for secular communication, D-A, taking out the beginning of the tale)."

Coyote: "I get it. Here's where the *meme* kicks in. Made aware of the danger, the man caps each end of the drum with a stone, impervious to arrows as well as sight (CANCELLATION E, E-B: stone for tympanum, opening or entering of drum. The little man's chosen medium for miscommunication has been OBVIATED. But now, as the man carries him off to be released, the little man invokes the final means of sound-communication, *command* (CANCELLATION F, F-C, SPARAGMOS: death on command for eye-death)."

Roy: "OBVIATION. NOT A for NOT D, MEME for DREAM. The little *man* effectively changes places with the surviving human being, ordering him to replicate on his own person the indignities that the little man has suffered (removing his hair and clothing to represent removal of the pandanus pod, cutting his earlobes to represent the drum, and cutting his nose and penis, appendages locally associated explicitly with *arrows*). Oh isn't life wonderful, Coyote?"

Coyote: "*In Jena geht Es wunderlich!* SUBLATION: THE STOP BUCKS HERE! Even the little man, seen before up on the mountain, is now gone."

Roy: "And his name was Pozhubo: 'He speaks EXCLUSIVELY.'"

Coyote: "*Das ist buchstabirt H E G E L auf Deutsch!*"

Roy: "*Und zwar L A E R T E S auf Änglisch.*"

Coyote: "You didn't bother to translate."

Roy: "Nor shall I; it is *selbstverstandlich*. At Harvard they told me I *must* learn German if I wanted to be an astronomer."

Coyote: "And look where it got you, Roy: the MEME, the secret dream of all anthropologists, the DATA that kicks your ass, gets up, walks by itself, talks by itself, and GETS A LIFE of its very own."

Roy: "The TONAL: you can dress it up, but can you *take it out?*"

Coyote: "You'll never get lonely on dates anymore."

Roy: "*I* drink To make OTHER PEOPLE more interesting."

Life on the Edge: The MEME that's on the BEAM

Coyote: "The strange and wonderful story of Ella."

Roy: "If she had anything, she had *edge*."

Coyote: "She positively *sparkled*."

Roy: "Negatively, too. What folktales miss in the process of institu-tionalization, or what could be called *de-naturing*, is the cutting edge of *risk* or *charm*, which turns what Don Juan calls *intent* into its object."

Coyote: "*Once upon a time* what we now think of as myths or folk-tales were *creative instruments of intent*, actual *spells* through which unbelievable transformations were brought about."

Roy: "Sonnets. WEAPONS."

Coyote: "In cases of extreme overfamiliarization, like the story of

Cinderella, the tendency is to overcompensate this loss with attribution of magic, caricature, sentimentality, and much worse."

Roy: "The details of the plot and characterization are well known, and for our purposes all that is necessary is to isolate the axes of cross-axial cancellation (D-AJ E-B, and F-O), noting only that, as usual, each SUBSTITUTION includes a great deal of subsidiary incidentalization."

Coyote: "Thus we have D-A: godmother-stepmother (coach-pumpkin, horses-rats, FOOTmen-mice); E-B, midnight at the Ball, down among the cinders (chafing debutante–desprized stepdaughter, no time left, all the time in the world, glitterati-household vermin); F-C: glass slipper-slip glasser narcissism (transparent footwear—self-adulation in mirror, splendid-attire-rags, exclusion of inclusive Ella, inclusion of exclusive Ella). In short, we have a BALL."

Roy: "In long, we have a HALL."

Coyote: "Yah, tell me about it: 'RATS—wrong FOOTman,' 'stroke of midnight—stoke at midday,' 'let's see some PRINTS—let's be some CHINTZ.'"

Roy: "In cases like this the only real way to rescue the Edge of Intent is not only to tell the tale backward, but re-conceive it entirely on that MEME:

SPLINTERELLA

Once, in a room made of glass, in a tower made of glass, in a palace made of glass, in a kingdom made of glass, lived a LASS made of glass. She could see through everything—even her parents were trance ones, like a transom over the glass door, and all she had for company were some PRINTS made by a muddy foot. She longed for the earth, and the cinders, and the RATS.

Way down below she saw a BALL, which could be the earth, so she danced with delight, leaving non-PRINTS all the way, till it got to be day. At the crack of dawn, down on the lawn. And down on the ground, all spinning around, from out of the clay, came a negative image, that looked like a scrimmage. It was her

HAIRY SOD MOTHER! She marshalled her forces, instead of coach-horses, said RATS, and sang her magic song:

What shall we do with a drunkin punkin,
What shall we do with a drunkin punkin
what shall we do with a drunkin punkin
Ear-lai in the morning?

Way, hey, and UP she rises,
Way, hey, and UP she rises,
Way, hey, and UP she rises,
Ear-lai in the morning.

And down came the glass, which fell on its ass, and down came the tower, at that very bitching hour, and down came the splinters, which fell among the cinders. And down came her fella, and he called her SPLINTERELLA.

And out of the fella she made her some PRINTS, and out of the blisters she made her some sisters. She slept with the PRINTS, and made him a father, she slept with the sisters and burned them to cinders. And all through the winters she gouged them with splinters—no mother, no father, no fuss and no bother, no RATS and no cats and no bats in the belfry. No one thing, no OTHER, no HAIRY SOD MOTHER—SHE'S DOWN IN THE DUST AND SHE *LIKES* IT THAT WAY! Till one day, unknowing—the embers were glowing—emerged just the mate she had wanted always. A SCARY CLOD BROTHER, proceeded to smother, her hopes and her fears and her frightful INCEST. He blew in her ear, and he bloodied her nose, and he dressed her all up in the fanciest clothes."

Coyote: "Hoo boy, Roy, you just RECTIFIED my whole life.
 (sings): 'Hey, BABA YAGA, hey, BABA YAGA . . .'"
Roy: (from a letter by Professor James Frederick Wiener to the author) "The trouble with OBVIATION, Roy, is that it SCARES people."

Coyote: "Hmmmm—Mahatma Gandhi, Wallace Stevens, Groucho Marx—*scars* them, too. Look what you done to their MYTH, Roy. Why *reconceive* a story backwards when the same set of oppositions is driving it forward?"

Roy: "That, my friend, is the Golden Section secret of psychoanalysis and the kind of retrospective view you get of a dream when you try to tell its story to yourself afterward. It's just as the poet Howard Nemerov said: 'The interpretation is the next room of the dream.'"

Coyote: "So you are both trying to get the gist of what Freud called 'the *dreamworker.* '"

Roy: "Precisely. The one who dreams you is exactly the same as the one you dream—regardless of whether that dream is a psychoanalytic trance-formation, a myth, a symphony, or even a *sonnet*. It is a self-aware manifestation of what Don Juan called The Definitive Journey."

Coyote: "If you can dream it UP, you can dream it DOWN."

Roy: "The MEME, the AUTOMIMETIC AGENCY, as we have seen, will take any guise necessary to lure you into that journey—the LUMINOUS EGG or COCOON, the LUCID DREAM, sometimes a *sonnet*, more often the kind of LUMINOUS MUSIC we get from very special composers such as Jan Sibelius or Antonio Vivaldi."

Coyote: "*Il Prete Rosso*, they called him, 'The Red Priest,' the red-bearded *dreamworker* from Venice . . .

Roy: " "Ah, *Venezzia* (background music, Vivaldi's *Concerto per Trombo Marina in C*).

Il Prete Rosso

All cats make secrets, taking down their minds,
which we make up for them, domesticate.
As horses do for violins, they mate
in tandem with the strutting of *behinds*,
the afterlife of cat—eviscerate.

So music makes its cause of double-binds

and double-stops behind Venetian blinds;
they also serve who only counter weight.
No sweep of bow but makes the stallion groan,
a lente, lente, currite, what's your hurry?
You be the judge, and I shall rape the jury.
His beard was red, but mind the undertone,
felicitatis nocte, soft and purry,
No cat but keeps a secret of its own.

Coyote: "Dennis the Menace from Venice."
Roy: "Venison, son: it's where the BUCK stops."

ACOUSTIC SUBLATION

Coyote: "DEER POWER is the most careful, courteous, and pre-
scient power known. SUBLATION—'The Stag at which your
Lordship every winter shoots'—is completely indefinable, arrested forever in the twilight between life and death. It stays forever at the point of its own transilience."
Roy: "Rilke, in the third sonnet of the second part of *Sonnets to
Orpheus*, speaks of mirrors as 'wasters of the empty gallery,
when the twilight happens, wide as the woods,' and of the chan-
delier, or *luster*, that 'goes through the impenetrable twilight of
the mirrors like a seventeen-point buck through the forest at
dusk.'"
Coyote: "We have heard that the intimately translucent Fifth Symphony of Sibelius was the consequence of a kind of shamanism—soul-capture of the composer by the wild swan. *Seven* of
which you saw at Porvoo, Finland, remember?"
Roy: "But we can only guess that the magnificently autumnal Seventh is the *hoabidi* of forest itself, a powerful, ancient stag har-
monizing death and the rutting season in a long, full sweep
of melody. That the main theme (trombones, marked *sonore*

in the score) is likely the grandest symphonic theme ever
conceived—

They Buck against the Wind
quasi una fantasia

Though all we know of motion makes a liar
of languages, and music moves too slow,
and day mates night in equinoctial fire—
they buck against the wind and sideways go.
And elegant, the stars the birches sire,
decamping in a swath the autumn blow—
the slate of spreading lakes like smoke below,
they buck against the wind and sideways go.

The ghosts of sun and shade, the shattered choir,
the sidelong buck that, slantwise with desire,
remodels wind in whistling to the doe—
the night above the lake like undertow—
where galaxies like hooded owls conspire
and buck against the wind and sideways go."

Coyote: "In the final analysis, both music and shamanism, like life-
forms themselves, are basically kinesthetic phenomena. What is
going on in the Fourth and Seventh symphonies is far too serious to be either joyful or tragic, and even philosophy, with its
static questions, is shaken and overcome."
Roy: "You forget yourself. This is a *stag*, as the English poet
Thompson put it, 'A stag of warrant, a stag, a stag / a runnable
stag with kingly crop . . . ' A *buruhoa* in self-inverted double
perspective, like what the New Ireland people call a *malanggan*."
Coyote: "In that case, let me try:

Stag Party
by Coyote

The moon's a swollen stag that walks the sky
and bugles hollow down the white-boned cliffs,

and flakes the fragile chalky shale, and sniffs
fermenting brooks and fields-of staring white
transparent grapes like globes of sleeping light
and thickets cobwebbed silver in his eye.

He tilts his gleaming tines to chase his does
through groves of ash and blowing beech and pine
and curves his supple new moon silver spine
above their backs in grottoes where he ruts
and valleys full of rotting wine and nuts,
the whirling milkweed breath he coughs and blows

will spray the slopes with golden seed-dust soon
and banks where leaves like rusty jewels fall,
the trombone shudder of his harem-call
will echo through the forest hollows long
and turn to frost as does the cricket's song,
sung soft beneath the mating of the moon."

Roy: "Yechhh . . . florid, heavy *romanticism*; I can imagine even
    Elgar and Rachmaninoff puking in the aisles!"
Coyote: "What? And not from the *podium*? Well, that's a *change*.
    But it's also the point of *Coyote Anthropology*: without the es-
    trangement of purely self-serving ornamentation, Roy, no expla-
    nation in the world is worth the effort of even *spitting* at it."
Roy: "SUBLATION—the 'stag at which your Lordship every win-
    ter shoots,' is completely indefinable, arrested forever at the
    midpoint between life and death—it stays forever at the point of
    its own transilience."
Coyote: "Like that mysterious IT that the caretakers were afraid of
    at Sibelius's home, Villa Ainola? The one that grabbed you twice
    in the pit of the stomach in 1999, when you were visiting that
    hermetic solitude."
Roy: "It felt like G-force, and knocked the wind out of me."
Coyote: "*Wood*-wind?"
Roy: "*Soul* wind: 'it unexists to bring the rest to life.' Sibelius was
    convinced that the different musical keys had concrete color-

values. D major was ochre yellow, and F major was metallic
dark green—like the tiles on the magnificent Finnish stove
in his dining room, one of the places where the G-force
grabbed me."

Coyote: "Music feels *you* in the gut! That was the stove in which,
one night in the 1940s, Sibelius burned the never-to-be-revealed
scores of three unpublished symphonies and twenty tone po-
ems, as a conducting student of Thor Johnson told you back in
1957."

Roy: "That, according to Victor Sanchez, is what the Indians of
Mexico call 'telling the story of your life to Grandfather Fire': A
recapitulation of The Definitive Journey."

Coyote: "So—what was the *second* time you got grabbed by the
ghost-that-was-not-a-ghost?"

Roy: "See, they had not disturbed the blankets on the cot in Sibelius's study, where he died in 1956. Secretly, when no one was
looking, I touched them, and ZOWIE! I was *arrested*. I went
into the kitchen, which was furnished in 1950s decor, just like
my parents' kitchen in Cleveland, where I had first heard the
Fourth Symphony on a little plastic radio. I was *floored*; I went
into immediate *recapitulation*."

Coyote: "Roy's *backward-Cinderella* story; PRAGMATIC OBJEC-
TIVITY—the tree that is neither its own shadow, nor the tree
itself . . . "

ROY: "That does not even begin to describe it.

Symphony #4 in A Minor

A symphony is too remote to cry,
the thought of sound unblinking is absurd,
apology is silence. Undeterred,
emotion fills the space that asks it why,
that cannot tell the listened from the heard
unspoken sound, Statistics is the lie
that number makes of quality; the eye
will never see the substance of the word.

The sun that walks the birch trees through the ways
that shadows make to hide reflection's pause.
The ghost of loneliness, the wraith of haze,
the red of passion's voice when life withdraws,
the frost that covers stillness with its gauze,
the space between the stars that night displays."

Particle Degradation: The FACT of Representation

Coyote: "The crisis that came upon Sibelius during the composition of his Fourth Symphony was something much larger than
the 'mid-life crisis' that may have afflicated him at the time."

Roy: "The so-called winter pastorale; 'alone with nature's breathing
things,' as Rosa Newmarch put it. The crisis between orchestral
over-decoration and the effective *nature* of physical reality."

Coyote: "It was far more than that, something that Goethe had set
in motion with his re-grounding of nature-knowledge on holographic principles, 'to bring it closer to the meaningful.' It was
the crisis of *representation* itself, the quintessential split between
the grandiosely aesthetic and the acutely scientific."

Roy: "Each being the result of false claims made upon the other.
Like the best *fiction* approaches, the acute *objectification* of science as a limit, whereas the best *nonfiction* 'reads like a novel,' as
they say."

Coyote: "No anthropologist has ever *seen* or *experienced* a society,
a culture, or even the *people* they were working with. Even in
the most intimate details of their interaction with those people,
not to speak of recorded notes or what is called 'theory,' *all the
anthropologist ever experiences is a REPRESENTATION of the
people or culture they PRETEND to study, as well as of themselves
representing that representation.*"

Roy: "No artist or scientist has ever seen, experienced, or even *intuited* the *object*, let alone the *subject*, of their representations,
but only the action, or working-out, of the process of representation itself."

Coyote: "That was the essence of Niels Bohr's *Copenhagen Decla-*

ration: that experiments performed *out of scale* with the abilities of *human* beings to make them meaningful *on their own scale* of experiential reality are doomed to a bizarre sort of *cognitive dissonance* or *self-dyslexia* akin to Heisenberg's Uncertainty Principle, or the quizzical thought experiment known as Schrödinger's Cat."

Roy: "It goes to the principle of *magnification*, the basic tool used for generations by natural scientists in all disciplines. As Goethe put it, '*telescopes and microscopes magnify the insignificant*.' Most of the distant galaxies we can observe are *empirically* smaller than germs, whereas, as an American poet put it, 'electrons deify a razor-blade into a mountain range.'"

Coyote: "The idea of the *particle* as a *basic constitutive unit* (or of the *unit* as a *particle*) *either* of matter/energy reality or of the way it must be represented, plays a strangely ambivalent role in this, a sort of zero-sum determiner, or subject/object *shifter*."

Roy: "What I have elsewhere described as *particle degradation*—the subliminal decay of *the represented* into *the field of representation*—and vice-versa. Self-inverting double perspective."

Coyote: "On the strictly experiential, or *plain-sight empirical* scale, physical and representational value-attributions change places when the tolerance limits of ambiguity are reached. Imaginably physical particles degrade into quizzical and even droll parts of the lexical inventory-sound-values like 'quark,' 'neutrino,' and 'gauge boson.' Whereas the conventional items of vocabulary turn into grotesque, particle-like units—phonemes, morphemes, sememes—when disconnected from meaningful statements at the microscopic level."

Roy: "*Lak mamaran*, 'luck in the double-focus.' New Ireland *malanggan* carvers create their surrealistic masterpieces '*To Remember the Faces of the Dead*,' as Tom Maschio so eloquently put it."

Coyote: "So they might as well have been representing *you*, eh? Great symphonies turn into *sonnets*, and these turn into pure conceits about the role of *sound* in naming and educing the facts of empirical reality."

Roy: "Funny you should mention that, for it brings us back to the details of Sibelius's compositional crisis, the *brute facts* of subliminal representation. The crisis that physics experienced about the matter-energy SUBLATION that resulted in Planck's quantum hypothesis, occurred at the same time—roughly 1900—as Heinrich Schenker's *holographic* theory arose about the germ-motif and its iterative self-interference patterning in classical music."

Roy: "The study of nature, on one hand, and the close examination of musical culture on the other, were approaching the same ends by different *means*. The Sibelius crisis, which actually lasted from 1911 to 1919, existed at a point of cross-fertilization between the two—roughly coincident with Einstein's work on Relativity."

Coyote: "Like my Stag, eh? Or like Dylan Thomas: 'My craft, or sullen art, exercised while the moon rages.'"

Roy: "Or like W. B. Yeats: 'Woven of the light and the half-light.' Schenker's claims that music's holographic underdeterminations are in fact *life-forms* in their own right are OBVIATED in the quasi-naturalistic realizations of Sibelius's works (swans, stags, cold red suns), which are in fact stupendous representations of *sound in its own body*."

Coyote: "Whereas, on the other hand, photons, quarks, neutrinos, and gaugebosons are *misrepresentations* of the sound-values that constitute their only reality."

Roy: "There is no such thing as a *single* sense; the fact is that the senses must imitate one another in order to apprehend their own values as such, that is, the sonnet of the symphony, and the symphony of the sonnet."

Coyote: "That thing, call it IT or whatever you will, which can imitate you better than you could ever imitate it, can also imitate *itself* better than itself could imitate itself."

Roy: "IT marks the point of closure between any conceivable representation and any conceivable reality . . . *each being the result of false claims made upon the other."*

Collective Expersonation that Takes on a Life of Its Own

Coyote: "Of all the structures, cultures, laws, constitutions, social organizations, and ways in which the forms and values of society are shared collectively among individuals . . . "

Roy: "All the ways in which the expersonative means of OBVIATION may be *impersonated* . . . "

Coyote: "Musical scores, literary texts, codicils, equations, periodic tables, artificial models or matrices of cosmic or national law or order . . . "

Roy: "Descriptions of things and of people, histories, genealogies, grammars, syntaxes, languages . . . "

Coyote: "Coyotes . . . "

Roy: "Coyotes . . . "

Coyote: "No static form of any kind carries the slightest hint of the *impetus."*

Roy: "Or holds in evidence any trace of the SUBLATION, of the *motion,* not to speak of the *motivation* that brought its *conception* into being in the first place."

Coyote: "Life in one long sentence."

Roy: "The *definitive journey* in one long OBVIATION."

Coyote: "Even the *derivative* in calculus is a contradiction in terms, dividing by zero, making a *positive* attribution of what amounts to speed or velocity in zero time (*no time* at all)."

Roy: "NOT DOING; the *extensional* quality of space has been OBVIATED, given that we measure the time factor by putting the temporal interval *in the denominator,* in this case dividing by *the difference between extension and itself."*

Coyote: "The NOT DOING of the calculus works in a dimension *that is perpendicular to time."*

Roy: "The calculus of OBVIATION works in a dimension that is perpendicular to *extension* in all its forms."

Coyote: "The *structure* of OBVIATION is the OBVIATION of structure."

Roy: "So any static structure or design, whatever its origin or purpose, is likewise a palpable *fiction* or a fantasy based on the potential arrest in space and time of the OBVIATIONAL process that brought it into being in the first place."

Coyote: "They BUCK against the wind and sideways go."

Roy: "There is no Hamlet quite like Hamlet, not even Hamlet himself."

Coyote: "Life is NOT a stage, and we are NOT merely players."

Roy: "We are LUMINOUS BEINGS conceived in dreaming and merging eventually with the *background* of the dream. Like the Daribi *buruhoa*, and like what the Australian aborigines call THE DREAMING, or 'dreamtime.'"

Coyote: "Dreaming is EXPERSONATION, SUBLATION is EXPERSONATION, and all we know of secular life is an IMPERSONATION."

Roy: "The most outrageous form of social organization ever conceived is that of the Meso-American *warriors' party*—a severely regimented *anti*social organization whose whole purpose and goal is the OBVIATION of its worldly and other-worldly status. It is to EXPERSONATE individuality itself and fuse into a single BEING."

Coyote: "Like a *corporation* that really lives up to its promises, it actually *becomes* the LOGO of its self-imaged advertising."

Roy: "CEO, Coyote: CONTROLLED EXPERSONATIONAL ORGANIZER."

Coyote: "In that case the LOGO would be the HUNAB KU working in a dimension that is perpendicular to what Don Juan calls *the axis of perception*."

Roy: "The HUNAB KU is a highly *abstract* imaging of the basis of ail perception, representation included. As a mutual overlapping, or in fact occlusion or 'eclipse' of the first and second attentions by one another, it belongs to neither and is in fact a visual impossibility showing what that occlusion would *mean* when seen from the vantage point of the THIRD ATTENTION."

Coyote: "Which automatically *kills* you, or comes upon you at the point of death, if you even try."

Roy: "The *death parallax*: to *burn with the fire from within*. If one were only able to sustain oneself, 'luck in the double focus.' Within that focus one would be able to *die and keep an awareness*, that is, treat even immortality itself as a sort of anticlimactic realization. But *don't hold your breath*, and be careful when crossing your eyes.'"

Coyote: "This happens to some people only inadvertently, through no 'fault' of their own, and is commonly known (which means basically *unknown*) as 'spontaneous combustion in human beings.' Rather contemptuously, Don Juan calls that 'the Eagle's Gift,' referring to the Meso-American conception of the super TONAL of all TONALs, the ultra-being called the EAGLE, which eats you when you die."

Roy: "Ectoplasmic endocannibalism; you are what you eat. Comes of insufficient detachment from the *description* or the items of the *inventory*. The EAGLE is made up of all the things that could not get past the EAGLE and died trying. EAGLE CITY is something like Las Vegas: what *preys* there, *stays* there. It's full of good advice, though, about how to get past the EAGLE."

Coyote: "Would you take it?"

Roy: "That would be like asking a gambler how he lost his chips. The EAGLE is actually a *hybrid* conglomerate made up of the quenched lifeforce elements of all aware beings in the universe that were not able to get past it. Don Juan: 'They float like barges on the *nagual*.'"

Coyote: "They buck against the wind and sideways go. 'So how *do* you get past the EAGLE?'"

Roy: "You 'win the lottery,' is what a gigantic redwood tree told a friend of mine in California. Don Juan says you can either do it by making a full and complete *recapitulation* of your life (like the Buddha did under the *Bo* tree), or by dreaming (making your physical body and your energy body into one and the same thing)."

Coyote: "But that is the exact description of the HUNAB KU."

Roy: "And an *inexact* description of the CORPORATION that uses the HUNAB KU as its LOGO."

Coyote: "So what is an EXACT description of the CORPO-
RATION?"

Roy: "The definitive journey of the warriors' party."

Coyote: "So I take it, from everything we've been saying in the past
few pages, that the party is a *picture* of the journey, and the journey itself is a *picture* of the party. So far, so good. But, Roy, what
exactly *is* a Warriors' Party?"

Roy: " A perfect miniature, or scale model of the human race, with
all the specific *roles* or attributes of its *types* of men and wom-
en moving in lockstep, fitting together like the pieces of a jig-
saw puzzle—a kind of self-unity that only clicks in when all the
component *roles* are moving in perfect *synch* with the totality."

Coyote: "So it's an *ideal type*: always right, never wrong, like the
U.S. Constitution, or what Lévi-Strauss calls an *elementary
structure of kinship*."

Roy: "That would be the biggest mistake you could make about it.
It is the OBVIATION of an ideal type—a structure that only *becomes* a structure when it works itself out in time and space."

Coyote: "So what is the basic *precept*, or historical model of the
Warriors' Party?"

Roy: "A subliminal text etched in the memory alone, verbalized
and objectified in Castaneda's book *The Eagle's Gift* as *The Rule
of the Nagual*. Don Juan says that the ancient seers picked it up
from 'the faint reflection of man in the EAGLE,' much as Chris-
tians claim that God wrote their Bible, or Hindus maintain that
their *Vedas* and *Upanishads* are implicit in the structure of the
universe."

Coyote: "And that model would be . . . ?"

Roy: "Well, it was not a model at all, just a kind of airplane-spot-
ter's manual, more or less, for the luminous bodies of the various types of men and women in their mutual intercalation into
a Warriors' Party. The problem with this is that second-attention
realities like the luminous body *make no sense* when translated
into the first attention, which is the only place where human beings can *think* or *reason* properly."

Coyote: "And that is why the seers of Don Juan's movement *made an interpretation,* and decided to 'treat the rule as a map,' or a *picture* of itself."

Roy: "And they didn't do such a great job of it, either. Too *mesmerized* by the inherently counterintuitive designs of the second attention. What they failed to take into consideration was the fact that this was not a *static,* but a *dynamic* structure—a 'map' of *movements* and *transformations.*"

Coyote: "Like the story of SPLINTERELLA: what they failed to take into consideration was the OBVIATION implicit in the Definitive Journey, the NOTDOING that is integral to the ways in which the various personifications of the Warrior' Party *must* interact with one another."

Roy: "They were not exactly *rocket scientists; clarity* may be 'almost a mistake,' but it's the only *clarity* we've got."

Coyote: "So in other words, the *roles* or *personifications* of the basic types of men and women only *come clear* when arranged in a perfectly synchronic schematic based on the NOT-DOING implicit in the HUNAB KU, the third attention mutual occlusion of the first and second attentions."

Roy: "Thus the Warriors' Party makes it through the passage, or gets past the EAGLE, by virtue of the *interference-patterning* between the first and the second attentions. Much as a Sibelius symphony makes it on the interference patterning among the holographic iterations of its germ-motif."

Coyote: "That means that the mysterious IT you encountered in Sibelius's home was grabbing at you from the Third Attention, like it actually *forced* you to write this text."

Roy: "It means much more than that. It means that the whole *origin* and *source,* as well as the *accomplishment,* of the Warrior's Party is based on the *fusion* and interference patterning of two remarkable BEINGS: the DOUBLE MAN and the DOUBLE WOMAN. 'Made *first* by the Creator to guide mankind to the passage, to *abstract* and *negotiate* the passage.'"

Coyote: "A DOUBLE BEING has two left sides and two right sides, like the Hindu goddess Kali, each *encompassing* the four polar types of its respective gender and thereby encompassing the whole Warriors' Party, both from within and without. I *got it*, Roy: *the Warrior's Party is itself the passage*, which is both created and negotiated by its own machinations from within!"

Roy: "Nice try, Coyote; close, but no cigar. The *machinations*, as you call them, are themselves a function of a much more encompassing figure-ground reversal, one that exercises its force from *both* sides of the EAGLE at once."

Coyote: "Knights, pissing in the shaft."

Roy: "The real SECRET behind the secret of the Warriors's Party is that they take the DOUBLE WOMAN, or NAGUAL WOMAN, of a given party *out past the EAGLE* with the exit of the PREVIOUS party, so she can act as a BEACON to the remaining members of her own, drawing them onward through the *Spannung*, or NOT-DOING tension between the Third Attention and its mere approximation on the other side."

Coyote: "So it's like the SUBLATION at the climax of Goethe's *Faust*: 'Die Ewig Weibliche zieht Uns hinan' (The eternal feminine draws us onward)."

Roy: "More like the perfect NIGHT TRAP, as navy pilots call it, on a storm-tossed carrier: *She* is the one called 'Paddles,' who guides you into a perfect landing."

Coyote: "Isn't it a version of that NOT-DOING tension that creates the design of the Warriors's Party itself? Who locks the respective 'four kinds of women' and 'four kinds of men' into their specific *roles*, *tasks*, and *identities*?"

Roy: "Sure is, and that's where the de facto interpretation of the rule, made by Don Juan's lineage 'screwed the pooch,' as navy pilots would say. They made a fatal mistake: they ignored the internal *cross-polarity* inversion among the four kinds of women, which are actually *eight* kinds of women arranged into two PLANETS, according to the Rule: the four kinds of *stalker* (first attention) women, and the four *opposite* kinds of *dreamer* (second attention) women. And thereby they missed the significance of the *tasks* of the four kinds of men.

Coyote: "Thus figure 8 is a RECTIFICATION of Don Juan's peoples' mistake?"

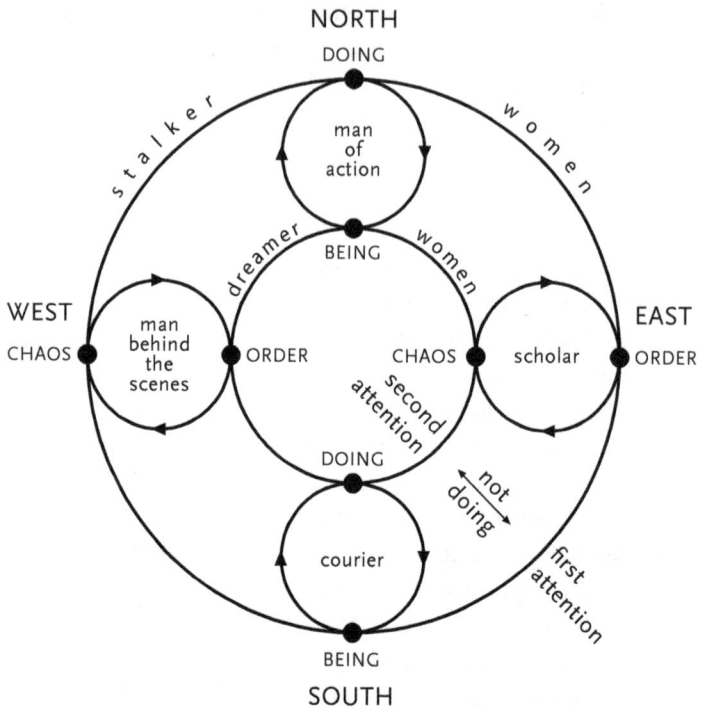

8. Rectified Schematic for The Rule of the Nagual

Roy: "Damn straight, *on your six*, Paddles! Those warriors were
unable to ENVISION the whole schematic precisely—couldn't
see the fourses for the threes, and now they're out there *spinning*
on some mad *recapitulation* of their own."

Coyote: "Correct me if I'm wrong, but the four poles of the diagram, assigning each of the *kinds* of women to one of the four
directions of Native American cosmology, ignore the fact that
there are two *different kinds of women* at that point, each *holding
the place* of the *oppositely* directed significance of the other. Like
they OBVIATE each other."

Roy: "Sure, the *north wind* woman is blunt and purposeful and
should be called DOING; her direction is *opposite* to that of
the *south wind* woman, who is warm and nurturing and called
'the Joker, the Warm Wind at your back' who should be called
BEING."

Coyote: "Like Marilyn Monroe. And the *east wind* woman, 'she is called ORDER,' is the 'Wind of Illumination' like the goddess Athena. Her direction, in its whole sense and semblance, is opposite to that of the *west wind* woman, called 'the spirit-catcher,' whose thing is CHAOS."

Roy: "Which is putting it mildly; she is prone to moods of manic depression and outright insanity, and *melancholia*. 'Warriors cry tears of blood,' as Don Juan put it."

Coyote: "Like your paternal grandmother, Roy, and like your wonderful green-eyed lover, 'Mother Right.'"

Roy: "Let's not get *personal*. These are immutable *types*, regardless of personnel changes, and the definitive work of the four kinds of male warriors can *only* be understood as that of *transacting* between two opposite polar types of women."

Coyote: "To be sure, the *man of action*, 'great, fickle, humorous companion (businessman); the *scholar*, 'honest and upright keeper of facts and histories' (subtle if you don't read close, Mr. Academic); the *courier* or *scout*, 'the type of assistant who has to be *told* what to do' (look him up on the Internet); and the *man behind the scenes*, 'the *unknown* and *unknowable* man' (spy, counterintelligence, anthropology), could not be made sense of in any other context than that of figure 8."

Roy: "Or, for that matter, in any context whatsoever in the case of the *man behind the scenes* since, according to the Rule, his body *involuntarily* emits a burst of CHAOS to keep the seer from *seeing* him."

Coyote: "The work or *task* of the *man of action* is to transact between the stations of the respective dreamer and stalker women at the top of the diagram, then turn second attention BEING into first attention DOING, where it *counts*. The work of the *scholar*, at the right, is to turn second attention CHAOS into first attention ORDER; the work of the *courier*, at the bottom, is to turn second attention DOING into first attention BEING, which is why, Marilyn Monroe or no, he has to be *told* what to do."

Roy: "And, last but not least, the work of the *man behind the scenes*, at the *left*, is, of course, to turn second attention ORDER into first attention CHAOS."

Coyote: "What Don Juan is doing here is something very special, something that is like backward OBVIATION. He is turning what seems to be an arbitrary *description*—such as 'ally' or sorcery implement—into a REALITY that happens precisely because you have taught yourself to feel it that way in your body."

Roy: "In his movement they call that 'making *your* command BE the EAGLE'S command,' but it is something that all human beings do unconsciously and inadvertently."

Coyote: "Hence the two key figures in the Warriors' Party are UN-MARKED in figure 9; the NAGUAL MAN and the NAGUAL WOMAN are *invisible* because they are the NOT-DOING of the whole thing. They are the *alpha* and the *omega* of the Definitive Journey."

Roy: "So we can think of the Warriors' Party and its definitive journey as the subliminal IMPERSONATION of the EXPERSONATIONAL design of the HUNAB KU—in which the transactional activities, or *tasks*, of the four kinds of male warriors both dramatize and mask the flux between the first-attention and second-attention images of the HUNAB KU. They trace out the otherwise invisible effects of the NAGUAL MAN in the design."

Coyote: "Whereas, of course, the outer circle of the *stalker women* and the inner circle of the *dreamer women* hold between them the precocious nuptial flight of the NAGUAL WOMAN to the other side of the passage. She is not *here* because she is *already there*."

Roy: "Just as Sibelius, or whoever that was, forms the invisible link between the first attention reality of his home and the never-neverland of the symphony."

Coyote: "AUTOMIMETIC AGENCY. You've really got to stop writing sonnets, Roy."

Roy: "In *The Power of Silence* Don Juan says the the Sorcerer-Storyteller 'attains his *whole perfection*' simply by the telling of stories, and then goes on to describe OBVIATION just as we have described it here. By that standard, making *my* command BE the EAGLE'S command, if I can get just one *sonnet* exactly right, or 'perfect,' I would need no Warriors' Party and no Definitive Journey. I would get off *scot* free."

Coyote: "Don't hold your breath."

Roy: "The sonnets *write me*, conceited though they be; just the perfect mate for a *narcissistic egoist*, with a God complex. You know what the Germans say about one of their greatest conductors."

Coyote: "'When God has delusions of grandeur, He dreams He is Herbert von Karajan.'"

Roy: "Yup. 'Forget the universe. HE controls the ORCHESTRA.'"

Coyote: "The DREAMING of the MEME-ing is the MEME-ing of the DREAMING. Don't quit your day job."

Roy: "The thing they call THE DREAMING forms the invisible link between the first attention secular reality of the Australian aborigines and the GREAT SPREAD OUT *NOW* of the Creative Epoch that some simplifiers have called the 'dreamtime.'"

Coyote: "Which the Walbiri people of central desert Australia call *djugurba*. They have it all—Warriors' Party, Definitive Journey, Passage, and the description that turns into stark reality because you have made it part of your body. They *live* and *think* that way."

Roy: "'Luck in the double-focus.' The strangest thing of all is what a Polish ethnographer told me in Vienna: 'The Walbiri *have* the ANTI-TWINS, Roy, *just exactly as you have described them.*'"

Coyote: "The strangest thing is that you keep writing almost-good *sonnets* when you could be out there kicking ass."

Roy: "I am of a naturally modest disposition, Coyote, subtle but demure, and most normally very, very *shy*. When God goes into a severe depression, He almost always imagines He might be me."

Coyote: "Tell me about it. The ABSOLUTELY strangest thing in the whole wide world is the totally impeccable match between the rectified version of Don Juan's Warriors' Party and the socio-spiritual schematic used by the Walbiri aborigines for every facet of their social and spiritual lives."

The Strangest Thing . . .

Roy: "It's like those famous last words: 'See ya on the FLIP side':

DE DREAMTIME LADIES SING DIS SONG
DOO-DAH, DOO-DAH,
DE DREAMING TRACK AM TEN MILES LONG
DID-JERIDOO DAH DAY,
WALK ABOUT ALL NIGHT,
WALK ABOUT ALL DAY,
AH BET MA MONEY ON DE RED KANGAROO,
SOMEBODY BET ON DE GREY."

Coyote: "What do you mean by FLIP, Roy, I mean besides being 'flipped out,' as usual?"

Roy: "I mean like DOWN UNDER, where the Australians live, the far side, you know, the funny edge—the ANTI-TWINS, the crack between the worlds."

Coyote: "It's gotta mean more than that."

Roy: "Afraid it does. It's the AUTOMIMETIC inversion, like the one we encountered in the physico-aesthetic phenomenon of *particle degradation* and the *medium steals the message* fact that the qualities and properties of *light*, in and of themselves, are alone responsible for the size and shape of the universe that we observe through them."

Coyote: "Well, what does it mean in *this particular contingency*?"

Roy: "It means that the very same diagram, first introduced by Claude Lévi-Strauss in *The Savage Mind*, can be used to describe both the rectified version of Don Juan's Warriors' Party in its Definitive Journey and the self-definitive life structure of the central desert aborigines. And with absolute conciseness in both instances."

Coyote: "Anthropology *does not exist*, Roy. Now, if you were selling used cars, that would be something, because cars *do* exist."

Roy: "Sure, Coyote; OBVIATION does not exist either, that is its POWER. Remember? Like John Donne might have said, 'And such a prescience doth the soul enjoy / it *unexists* to bring the rest to life.'"

Coyote: "So what is the relevance of the *soul*, or the AUTOMI-METIC INVERSION, or the ANTI-TWINS, *in this particular contingency*?"

Roy: "Well, the Walbiri told Mervyn Meggit that the whole system, which 'works like the windmill at the station,' was given to them by two birds: Wedge-Tailed EAGLE and Pink Cockatoo."

Coyote: "BIG BIRD, yet! Roy, as you yourself once put it, 'Humor explains NOTHING, it makes rather a *circus* of its relevance to the matter at hand.'"

Roy: "Oh YEAH? Take a good hard look, a 'squizzy,' as the Aussies would say, at figure 9. The figure marks the affinal, or marital, and also the descent-lineal, or cross-generational *substructure* of the *traditional* Walbiri social and spiritual organization. Each U-shaped figure (the traditional aborigine icon for a person seated on the ground, its 'track,' so to speak) marks the spot of one of the eight so-called SUBSECTIONS, defined in its place by both cross-generational *matrilineal* and *patrilineal* descent."

Coyote: "So then the curvilinear *dotted lines* on the figure would represent mutual affinal, or marriage connections between the respective SUBSECTIONS, grouped two by two—*they marry each other*. Like *Djambidjimba* and *Djabangari* on the diagram (right, inside), or like *Djungarai* (left, outside) and *Djangala* (top, inside)."

Roy: "As any FOOL can plainly see, SEE? It's like a NOT-DOING between the cross-generational *maternal* descent-line *Djam-bidjimba-Djabananga-Djagamara-Djungarai*, going *clockwise* around the outer circle, and its oppositely motivated other, the maternal descent line *Djangala-Djabaldjari-Djuburula-Djaban-gari*, on the inside track, going *counterclockwise* around the in-ner circle."

Coyote: "Aha—'De dreamtime ladies sing dis song'—the outer

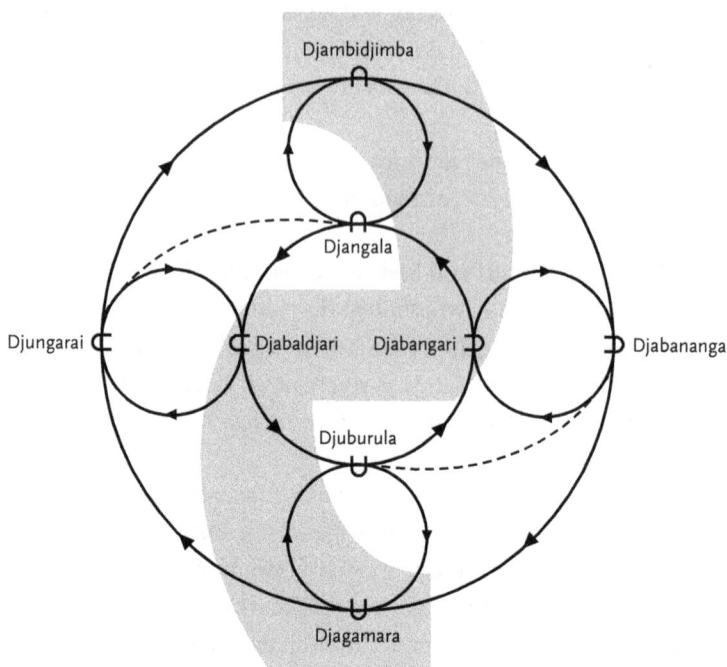

9. Walbiri Socio-Spiritual Organization, Shaded to Mark Wedge-Tailed Eagle Endogamous Patrimoiety

circle on figure 9 is like the ring of *stalker-women* in figure 8, the rectified version of Don Juan's Warriors' Party, each holding place at one of the four directions. And the inner circle is like the ring of *dreamer-women*, each doing the NOT-DOING of that direction."

Roy: "Oho—'*doo dah, doo dah*,' Lévi-Strauss calls these *cycles*, each circumventing the *whole* of the system in an opposite way, whereas the four cross-generational male descent lines he calls *couples, Djambidjimba-Djangala-Djambidjimba* (father-son-father-son) alternate by generative NOT-DOING between the contra-rotating *cycles* of the women."

Coyote: "So, HEY—the four *couples* are just *exactly*, by *position* and by *transaction*, like the *four kinds of men* in the Warriors'

Party, making their Definitive Journeys by turning one cycle of the women into the opposite signification of the other."

Roy: "Two by two, two by two, *everything* on the diagram works on the NOT-DOING principle of the ANTI-TWINS, even *in your dreams*. For the purely *secular* manifestation of the kinship-sequence is likewise used for *ritual* ('dreamtime') pairings and cross-pairings of the units, or separate *dreamings* as they call them."

Coyote: "'De dreaming track am ten MILES long,' just like the aniMILES going two by two into Noah's Ark."

Roy: "EXPERSONATELY speaking, that is, for the SUBSECTION identities were actually quasi-animal beings in the *dreamtime*, of which the people themselves are only IMPERSONATIONS, like the *four kinds of men* and the *eight kinds of women*."

Coyote: "Ah bet ma money on de red kangaroo'—that would be Pink Cockatoo, wouldn't it? Like the *sui-generis*, self-autochthonous, NOT-DOING male *endogamous* (that means 'marrying within itself') Semi-Moiety, that is *unshaded* in figure 9."

Roy: "'Somebody bet on de grey.' Nasty stuff. That would for sure be Wedge-Tailed EAGLE Semi Moiety, shaded *grey* on figure 9. It's like two NOT-DOING Warriors' Parties, *each BEING the result of false claims made on the other*, each making its separate bid for immortality, each trying to get past the other's BIG BIRD."

Coyote: "Like two chess players, each playing the *inside* of the other's strategy, even though the *Board* knows only one."

Roy: "'Why do you hate me, Roy, every time I *whip* you in one of our chess games?' *Perfect match*, for a narcissist with a God-complex. She had red hair, too, and green eyes, and when she was done gloating, she would go over and solve my Rubix Cube once again, for spite."

EVEN STRANGER: The Game of Chess

Coyote: "So every stag gets the *game* he deserves, eh Roy?"

Roy: "Chairman of the bored. Perfect *pointe d'appui* for thinking, and also doing—the game of life turned inside out. Every model for kinship or strategy can be modeled better on the chessboard. Even *mating*. Check it out: chess begins with two populations, evenly matched, like two Warriors' Parties each trying to get past the other's EAGLE, and proceeds turn by turn by dual by-play down to a single *mating*. Life begins with a single pair and proceeds, by dualistic foreplay, to a *full house*. There is the *life* of chess, and the chess of *life*, the strategy that anthropologists conceal from themselves when they think of it as *kinship*."

Coyote: "Chess only models what we might call the *difference* between the Warriors' Party and the traditional Walbiri socio-spiritual DREAMING scenario. You get what Don Juan calls the True Pair in all three cases: the NAGUAL WOMAN and the NAGUAL MAN, Pink Cockatoo and Wedge-Tailed EAGLE, and the self-inverted *battery* of the inset kings and queens—the only *gendered* pairing on the board."

Roy: "The four male *couples* in figure 9, and Don Juan's four transactional types of male activity (fig. 8), are *perfectly matched* in the game of chess. The *courier* or scout, 'the type of the assistant who must be told what to do'—those are the *pawns* who scout ahead of the Warriors' Party. The *rook* or castle, foursquare and solid, that's the *scholar*; the fickle *knight*, dancing between the squares, he's the *man of action*; whereas the *bishop*, slantwise in his action, conspiratorial, like the cardinals *Mazarin* and *Richelieu*, is the *man behind the scenes*."

Coyote: "Event *rules the game* in all three cases: getting past the EAGLE, merging with the *dreamtime*, and moving toward *checkmate*. But event itself is only the by-play of the four male types—transactors of the difference between the two sets of four place-holding women."

Roy: "But what about the eight types of women, the ones who hold *place* in the two diagrams, and are *held by* place?"

Coyote: "That's the real difference between the two diagrams, the normally invisible *framing* of the game; eight by eight is 64, and there are 64 squares on the chess-board."

Roy: "So then what is the difference between chess on one hand and the Warriors' Party and Walbiri system on the other?"

Coyote: "*Schachtspiel med Doden*—'chessplay with death,' as in Bergmann's *The Seventh Seal*. SYMMETRY and opposition—it's the *point* of our whole discussion. Chess has a single MEME, as if it were a single *strategy* that the two players compete for, and that takes them over by turns, whereas the Warriors' Party and the socio-spiritual schema are *collective* forms that involve the mutual integration of a number of MEMES."

Roy: "IT always wins, IT always loses. The STRANGER QUEEN, the part of us that loves the wind and the night and danger, the Splinterella AUTOMIMETIC AGENCY that anticipates itself so well that it acts perfectly, like a ballet dancer. And without even thinking—PURE ABANDON, future in its own past."

Coyote: "It has a single point, a single message, a single *motivation*, one that is so defeating to our Western minds that even the great Sigmund Freud was obliged to divide it in two—the life principle he called EROS and the death principle he called THANATOS—to even begin to make sense of it."

Roy: "Reason beyond reason: no tragedy so deadly but that it catches the edge of its irony, no humor so deliriously funny but that it finds itself transfixed on the point of its tragedy. The MEME of the goddess KALI, with her ghastly earrings—a dead infant depending from each ear—and her neck-lace of skulls, each one of them a letter of the Sanskrit alphabet."

Coyote: "Red hair and green eyes. 'Why do you hate me, Roy, when I beat you in one of our chess games?' She dances *victory* at the intersection point between past-in-its-own-future and future-in-its-own-past, between the *presence* and the *passage* of time."

Roy: "She SHINES, she SHINES like a *supernova* from the far side of Infinity! She's LIKE A RAINBOW."

Coyote: "So we have been OBVIATING the wrong play all along. It should have been *Romeo and Juliet*!"

Roy: "William Shakespeare, the REAL William Shakespeare, first got an *inkling* or striking-point of that message when he was an apprentice leather-worker (glover, like his father) in northern Italy, watching the *mayhem* of the Lombard street gangs.

Montagues and Capulets, *West Side Story*, GANGS OF NEW YORK."

Coyote: "The *glovers* of England at that time, according to Philip K. Bock, were *Lollards to a man*, that is, followers of that great contemporary of Chaucer, JOHN WYCLIFFE, who OBVIAT-ED the message of Martin Luther over a century beforehand."

Roy: "I like to imagine, in *Middle English* of course, what would happen if the great WYCLIFFE were miraculously transported across space and time to the sacred cenote at Chichen Itza, and made the Definitive Journey of the Mayan Prophet HUNAC CEEL, Ruler of Mayapan, who threw himself as sacrifice into the sacred waters and emerged triumphant, bearing the Proph-ecy of the Rain God, CHAC MOOL:

We Have No Need of the Visible Chirche

To given Rat's Ass for the Godde of Reyne,
hir Lollardye beliketh me in swoun,
hir Chirche Invisibel lay upside-doun
tho levere Elenor of Aquiteyn —
to amenuse, preche withouten soun,
ne Holy Aqualung to me susteyn
whilom I hadde watere on the brayn
and twenty fadom depe below the toun,

belike it were the Bathing Hous of Sodom,
Saintes and Martyr all about the bottom,
ab-hominable Messe everichoon;
I stonde her and no thing more to done,
the more he semeth, more he ben the same.
the more Invisibel — *I hadde Dreme*."

Coyote: "How many Martin Luthers can dance on the head of a pin? You ought to thank your teacher, *Bartlett J. Whiting*, the ex-pert on humor in Chaucer."

Roy: "He would only nod at me and smile when we passed on the

streets of Cambridge, as though he knew something that we
both could not fathom at that time."

Coyote: "And right after that, no doubt, it would *rain*. Meanwhile,
back at the *raunch*, as you Easterners are wont to say . . . "

Roy: " . . . We have this little thing about Romeo and Juliet, the
MEME of tragedy *miming* itself: All tragedy has a *motion*,
'e-motion without an e,' and in the great NOH dramas of Japan,
at the crucial time the performers will *strike the pose* of that motion while the musical accompaniment goes wild."

Coyote: "A tragic *stillicide*, as Nabokov would have it, that the
greatest melodist of all time, Serge Prokofiev, captured perfectly
in his ballet *Romeo And Juliet*:

Forget the contradictions, dance the FLAWS,
make music MEAN the way it should not go,
as lightning shakes its shadow-echo show
all melodies are humor without cause.
Imagine all the things you dare not know—
unthinkable, they also have their laws:
the love that really kills retracts its claws,
and hate has greater hatreds to forego.

Wolves mortify the stars with ultrasonics;
what music does for lovers goes by chance,
the practiced lie, and what that lie unsheathes,
dysharmony prefigured in the dance
like KALI's metaphor preserved in onyx;
no creature knows that innocence, and breathes."

Roy: "The best SUBSTITUTE for explanation, or death, which-
ever comes first, is to *say it all it once*, in pictures, with decorum,
with finesse, and with absolute finality."

Coyote: "But that runs the risk of *mistaken identity*, as with Hamlet, Pozhubo, and Splinterella, bless her buttons. Re-enchanting
the disenchanter: getting *someone else* to commit one's suicide,
like Hamlet and Ophelia or Romeo and Juliet."

Roy: "The imitation of love is the love of imitation."

Coyote: "And that goes double: 'luck in the double focus' for egoistic narcissists like you, and, of course, Pygmalion. I have, if you and Bartlett J. Whiting don't mind, a little poem written all by myself that I have been saving up for this occasion:

Coyote's Poem

Pygmalion made a *statue* and she called him Bernard *Shaw*,
she had him by the *short hairs* and he wore them on his *jaw*,
the two became a *marvel*, and the *one* became a *play*
he carved it out in *marble*—you can see it to this *day*.

The Greek is to his *statue* as the writer to his *ink*,
the body is an *image* that the mind can never *think*,
not *much* is left of *passion* when it *makes it* through the *eye*,
and the COYOTE is the JACKAL he outFOXES on the SLY."

Roy: "Well, it *worked*. You got me DOUBLED UP, and not with LAUGHTER either."

Coyote: "Good. And now for the tender-LOIN."

Roy: "TENDER-loin? What the HELL might *that* mean?"

Coyote: "Well, if we was *Sasquatch*, it would mean NAWK, because NAWK means 'friend' in their language—*which we are not supposed to know*—so in this case it means NOO YAWK."

Vikings, Toasting the Millennium, Down by the Battery

Roy: "Which Millennium?"

Coyote: "Why, the only one appropriate to their occasion: The FIRST Millennium."

Roy: "With *aquavit*?"

Coyote: "*Line aquavit*, the *Norwegian* kind that has to make it across the *line*, or, in other words, the *equator*. See, there is much we do not know about the early Norse presence in the Americas, including how far they got."

Roy: "On the first date?"

Coyote: "More likely the first *pineapple*, or *cashew nut*. There are murals in the *Temple of the Warriors* at Chichen Itza of white-skinned, blond-haired captives held down over sacrificial altars, and red-bearded captives being led in shackles, with a *ship* in the harbor bearing a sail . . . "

Roy: "There were no *sails* in the New World!"

Coyote: "Nor *line aquavit* either, until the Norse got there. The recovered remains of Norse settlement in the New World, at L'Anse aux Meadows, dated at about 1000 AD, show an *exploration site*. They had *smithies* there, and *shipyards*, and *nuts* brought from up the St. Lawrence."

Roy: "And they certainly damn well knew about the Millennium, and had a certain *affection* for strong drink."

Coyote: "It's more than that. Studying the texts of the *sagas*, a Norwegian expert determined that the only place an the eastern seaboard that exactly matched the description of Leif Ericsson's settlement in the New World was NOO YAWK harbor! Dig down under all the English and Dutch debris down at the Battery, or the 'Collect' at Five Points, and you'll find their smashed drinking cups."

Roy: "Skoll!"

Coyote: "LUCK IN THE DOUBLE FOCUS! (sings):
Noo Yawk, Noo YAWK,
it's a wonderful town,
the Bronx is up,
and the Battery's down."

Roy: "Well, *your* battery may be low, like your sense of humor, but I hear BANJOS."

Coyote: (sings, with banjos):
Ah couldn't find no RAINBOW,
ah got no pot of gold,
so ah come down to Hell's Kitchen,
where drunks and joints are rolled,"

Both: "TO ME WAY-A, SANDY, MY DEAR ANNIE,

OH, YOU NEW YORK GALS,
CAN'T YA DANCE THE POLKA?"

Coyote: "Say now, Roy, ah been wonderin'—why do they call New York the Big Apple?"

ROY: "Comes from understanding things the wrong side up."

Coyote: "OVER-standing?"

Roy: "You got it, Babe!
   And when I rolled around the town
   they showed me for a freak;
   I vested out my transfer then
   and turned the other cheek,"

Both: "TO ME WAY-A, SANDY, MY DEAR ANNIE,
   OH, YOU NEW YORK GALS,
   CAN'T YA DANCE THE POLKA?"

Coyote: "Like rosy cheek apple, hey, seen from the wrong side up?"

Roy: "Keep your *vest tight*, Buster. The Big Apple metaphor stems from New York street slang in the 1860s. Back then they used to call Manhattan Island 'The Frog and Toe.'"

Coyote: "Like 'Frog and Toe and AWAY WE GO?'"

Roy: "Nope. Comes from looking at a horse's hoof from the bottom. See, the soft, inner part—the *tenderloin* as it were, like the brothels and pubs in the inner part of the island—that's the FROG. And the hard outer shell—like the ring of docks and longshoremen around the periphery—that's the TOE."

Coyote: "So in my lady's apron
   I wandered most forlorn,
   till MARTIN CHURCHILL took me in,
   and he sent me round Cape Horn."
   (HIGH CAMP—B A N J O crescendo)

Both: "TO ME WAY-A, SANDY, MY DEAR ANNIC,
   OH, YOU NOO YAWK GALS,
   CAN'T YA DANCE THE P O L K A?"

Coyote: "Ah still don't git it, Roy. where does the BIG APPLE come IN?"

Roy: "It's not where it *comes in* that counts—STRAIGHT FROM THE HORSE'S MOUTH—but where it *goes out.* You can look a GIFT HORSE in the mouth all you want, but when you're in the FROG AND TOE, you better *mind the other end,* friend."
Both (slammin' banjos): "C O Y O T E A N T H R O P O L O G E E E E E!!!" *EXEUNT SALTANT*

Who would believe there's a pot of gold at the end of a RAIN-BOW? Which end? Is it like a mirror, that uses the possibility of an *inside* to distract that of an *outside*, and vice-versa? Surely there must be something there, but where, exactly, is 'there?' It was with thoughts like these that Coyote pursued his course, or maybe it was the other way around. "Not a RAINBOW in sight. Gotta keep lookin'"; and he went on and on.

Now who was it said that thing about "the wrong war, at the wrong time, in the wrong place, and with the wrong enemy?" Coyote had a certain dyslexia about everything—his thoughts and movements as well as meteorological phenomena—and he lost his footing and fell into what is known in those parts as an OXBOW LAKE. He couldn't tell one BOW from another, and besides, it was *dark* down there and hard to see. Finally Coyote did make out something. "And who might you be?"

"I'm the kind of gal you meet when you go looking for RAIN-BOWS and then fall into an OXBOW LAKE."

"Oh, there is so much I need to learn from you. For instance, what exactly is a pot of gold, and which comes first, the right or the left?"

"Look, Mister, I'd be glad to tell you *anything*, if you will just kindly let me know WHAT THE HELL HAPPENED TO MY SHEEP."

Roy: "It is not *what* you say, but *how you say it* that counts—the voice, the character, the precise *underdetermination* of your words."

Coyote: "I beg to differ. It is what you *really* say that counts most—the *overdetermination* of *fact* behind the pictures we make of it."

Roy: "You're *both* wrong. The underdetermination of overdetermination, or vice-versa, is merely a battle of *rhetorics*—the politics of representation. The best we can hope for is to bring these two into SYMMETRY or *equilibrium* with one another; the *balanced* fact, the *balanced* line."

Coyote: "The *cause* of the *effect* meets the *effect* of the *cause*; and at that point of suspension—what Don Juan calls 'stopping the world'—the humorous and the serious meet and merge with one another. You know, Roy, you human beings are the craziest critters in the world. You honestly believe you can *detach* yourselves from that SYMMETRY and still have your way."

Roy: "I wouldn't talk, Coyote."

Coyote: "We come to a point where the difference between organic and inorganic SYMMETRIES disappears—the *vanishing point* between what the old anthropologists used to call 'nature' and 'culture.' All 'cultures' merge with one another—as you say, *holographically*—and so, in fact, do all 'natures.'"

Roy: "The anthropologist wants to be the *figure* as well as the *ground*. And so, in fact, the figure-ground reversal itself honestly believes it is an anthropologist."

Coyote: "Though it is really the *interference-patterning* between the two that counts most: the way in which *any two* polarities interfere with one another."

SYMMETRIES

Roy: "We have studied biology as though it were evolution, and evolution as though it were biology. The one thing that matters most in determining the *environment* is the *species* that has created that environment through a process of mutual adaptation."

Coyote: "Add together *all* the species in that environment, in their communicative relations with one another, and you will have *said* something. They are not species at all, but *multivalent us-*

ages, part of the SPECTRUM of life-empowerment. They are SYMMETRIES that the *sonnet* captures in epigrammatic form."

Roy: "None of the so-called 'natural laws' can exist in isolated form, alone and by itself. In every instance where *gravity* (which the Germans call *Schwierigkeit* and the New Irelanders call 'female fight') has been used or observed, it contains a fractional coefficient of *angular momentum* (anti-gravitic *velocity*), just as angular momentum is nonexistent without the presence of gravity. Neither of these forces would matter in the slightest but for the electromagnetic SPECTRUM, the emissions of which are solely responsible for everything we know about natural forces or laws."

Coyote: "But without the *presence of mind*, the *sentience* determined upon the tuning fork-like *resonance* of the interference patterning between cause and effect, all the so-called 'forces' in the universe would go for nothing. Even *gods* would need the mute witnessing of the *sentient* to echolocate *what they are*, and how to differentiate themselves from one another."

Roy: "Or human *languages*, for that matter. Each language, to say nothing of the story-forms told within it—mirrors to its text—is a complete world in itself, constantly changing form and content. But each is likewise completely dependent on other languages outside of and within it, regardless of how isolated it may be. There is only *one story* in all of human history and synchrony."

Coyote: "And we are about to tell it."

Roy: "Don't hold your breath."

The Story

There is a very old story, at least twice as old as we are. It is the story of setting up the illusion of its own previousness to itself, as though it were born ass-backward and upside-down with the navel-cord wrapped around its neck. And the story goes like this: Way back in the beginning, MYTHS sat around the campfire telling PEOPLE to one another. And the MYTHS and the PEOPLE were each the better half of the others' illusions, *each being the result of false claims made upon the other.* And the stories would not die, for the life of the people caught within them. And the people would not really *live*, either, for the life of the stories caught within them.

Coyote: "Now that story tells me *nothing.*"

Roy: "Scant wonder. It OBVIATES the need for world-historical depth, as well as the distinction that is usually made between 'civilizations' and 'tribal' or 'primitive' cultures."

Coyote: "*And* human beings and coyotes."

Roy: "Don't bet on it:

Important that these sonnets have no order,
by random chance assortment is conferred,
important that the message go unheard,
important that creation has no border;
the sonneteer is just a minor third,
the singing line is but a tape recorder,
the Muse a happenstance of wild disorder,
important that the *sentence* be a *word.*

Significant, perchance, the suave comportment,
the chant of reason goes by happenstance;
illusion mates the mind with stiff cohesion,
the casualties of artistry are *lesion*;
incontrovertible, the weird assortment,
significant, you read it at a glance."

Coyote: "In *other words*, if you don't get the message, the MEDI-UM will surely get *you.*"

Roy: "And I, for one, am a HAPPY medium."

Coyote: "Take the inherent simplification of the heuristic as a factor in its own right, as something basic to understanding, and the whole significance of the *natural* as opposed to the *supernatural* disappears. Apart from the placement of its humanism, there is nothing primitive or unnecessarily anthropomorphic about Navajo thinking, and nothing obscurely Native American about the Navajo processing of thought."

Roy: "They know the ANTI-TWINS, after all, and they call them *Sa'a naghaii* and *Bik'e Hozhoo*, 'Lifetime Recursive,' and 'Referred Again to Itself as Excellence.'"

Coyote: "Would some traditionalist Navajo anthropologists studying the scientific world conclude that it is really a collection of moralistic tales about 'Force Man,' 'Perception Woman,' and the 'Matter-Energy Twins'?" Would they also observe, taking a glance at our consumer-fantasies, that we not only invent supernaturals of this sort, but want to eat them, like the rubbery pizza-people in commercials, mutilate them like crash-test dummies, and elect or impeach them like the caricatures in political cartoons? No wonder those old-time anthropologists had such trouble in defining the supernatural; we *use it to define ourselves*."

Roy: "In other words, why not treat the abstractions and principles of science as *people*, or personality profiles, since it is only people who know things, use them, and introduce knowledge of them to one another?"

Coyote: "Even if we do not connect *gravity* with the pompousness and grasping personality of Sir Isaac Newton ('attraction' would hardly be the word), or *evolution* with the ponderous lifestyle of Charles Darwin, we do dramatize the whole history of discovery and invention through the egos and interactions of the people involved in it. And since most of those inventors and discoverers are no longer around, it is left to the authors or lecturers who interpret them to give real *character* to the quality of scientific abstraction."

Roy: "For all of it is just simply people talking to people, and talk, or reading, is just a small part of what goes on in comprehension. Advertisers are the puppeteers of abstraction; they tell us that it is really the quality of life that matters, and take the abstract or super-personal distance of the product (it is *scientific*!), corporation, or logo, and turn it back into something that looks and feels like people. Only more so. The problem is that advertising has come to be such an art form, a product in its own right, that its modeling has the reverse-effect as well: it turns people into the products that consume them."

Coyote: "Or books about coyotes, eh?"

Roy: "Enough to make a pre-logical mentality think twice about it. Even at its worst, sorcery only tries to kill people, or make them sick. So maybe even *post-logical* folks like the Navajo knew all along that no abstraction of any kind, however deep, innovative, or useful, is worth anything more than the concrete imageries used to make sense of it. That the model does more for the mathematic than the mathematic can do for the model."

Coyote: "John Farella told you *that*?"

Roy: "John Farella was, by all the gods, the greatest student the Navajo ever had. Scientific agencies are *animated automation*; that is, the *presence of mind* in them recognizes its function as a *mechanical*, or thing-like agentive. Regardless of whether the subject matter is animate or inanimate, physical, chemical (ever meet a carbon-reaction that *didn't*?), biological, social, mental, or even literary, its model is machine-like and self-organizing in the way that we are to understand its workings. It is objective, tough-minded as they say. However, its impressions might be laundered back into the fuzzy-minded, impressionistic, or humanistic. Automation, the 'works by itself' overmodeling that we now demand of ourselves, comes out in the *wash* as the washing machine."

Coyote: "Like Don Juan said, we do not live the life of our emotions, but of the *description* of our emotions."

Roy: "And as the Irish would say, SYMMETRIES are what God made coyotes for."

Coyote: "And as Reilly said, 'Ukrainians did not learn to sing until they invented the washing-machine.'"

Roy: "Oh YEAH? 'Giddy-ai-ay, giddy-ai-ay, giddy-ai-ay for the One-Eyed Reilly.'"

Coyote: "BE SIRIUS! The form of agency that becomes thing-like *only to make its point*, like the animal-spirit guides, the mountain, the wind, the thunder people, the verbal spell or partici-patory ritual that effects a humanly-desired happening in the world, does this the opposite way around. It is *automated ani-mism*, and you have to do its work, pretend its fantasies for it. By *hand*, if necessary."

Roy: "Otherwise, and on the surface, there is not much difference between them. The logic that was primitive at its roots but has since grown up into objectivity and the *animism* that is really logical at its core are the same thing coming and going. They ef-fect the causes and cause the effects of one another. Why else would early pioneers like Edward Burnett Tyler and Sir James Frazer, to say nothing of Lucien Lévy-Bruhl, be so absolute-ly proud of what they had discovered as *animism*, the different ways that we and they think about it? The civilized folks ani-mate the proposition with what they can learn about how others think, and the others proposition the animal. 'Think like a horse to imagine where the horses have run off to' is how Evans-Pritchard put this, and he was being very droll."

Coyote: "This is absolute nonsense, Roy, and you know it."

Roy: "Get a good, hard grip on reality, *Die Wirklichkeit*, Coyote, you're gonna need it."

More Closely UNRELATED to Us than We Are to Ourselves

Coyote: "We have already been acquainted with some of the ways in which *extension*—space and time, to our rigid, compartmen-talized minds—is similar to itself, the kind of detached, out-of-body heuristic that topologists and fractal mathematicians call 'self-symmetry.'"

Roy: "We have encountered the first two examples of this: the Mo-bius Strip and the Klein bottle. If you recall, they were connect-ed with representation, memory, the Gimmick, Don Juan's con-ception of *seeing*, the *déjà vu* and the *vùjá de*, and thereby the highly counterintuitive facts of *incest* and *outcest*."

Coyote: "They are highly counterintuitive in the way that *repre-sentation* itself is, as in the Wittgenstein paradox: the fact that although 'what is reflected in language cannot be expressed by means of language,' that fact itself *must be expressed in language*, and is therefore true *because* it is false, and, of course, false *because* it is true."

Roy: "This alone gives us the confidence to re-state the first two examples of self-symmetry in highly abstract terms:

1. A Mobius Strip is an *axial* one-sided self-symmetry.
2. A Klein bottle is a *bi-axial in-sided* self-symmetry."

Coyote: "Furthermore, the experiences of Chapter 2 (the picture of the picture, the visual HUNAB KU) and of Chapter 3 (acoustical pictures in *sound*; the mutual interference-patterning between the visual and the acoustic; OBVIATION) give us the confidence to establish three more examples:

3. A mirror is a one-sided *visual* self-symmetry.
4. A Sibelius symphony is an *acoustical* one-sided self-symmetry, thereby OBVIATING the counterintuitive self-valuation of the emotions.
5. The difference between the waking and dreaming states of BEING is a self-axial *three-sided* self-symmetry, exactly as depicted in the HUNAB KU: the *first-attention* and the *second-attention* both *foregrounded* and *backgrounded* against each other, and the *third-attention* as the point of parallactic displacement between the two."

Roy: "I call that FIVE POINTS, Coyote."
Coyote: "And I call it the ANTI-TWINNING of SYMMETRY with duality. Each traps the other within itself and gives rise to a *third*, which is the point of OBVIATION for life's representation of itself to itself."
Roy: "The *recapitulation* of the first-attention within the dreaming state of the second-attention is called a *lucid dream*. That is in many ways the secret of all shamanism. But there is also the direct opposite of this in what Don Juan calls *dreaming*

awake—the recapitulation of the second-attention within the first that makes a cold, hard, *empirical* reality of the otherwise fuzzy and subjectively dissembling second-attention. Don Juan calls this *sobriety*, and it is like the objectivity of objectivity itself. The *ultimate* pragmatic."

Coyote: "That is the shamanism of the *Essences* that language makes of our world, the so-called *realism* of Plato's Cave analogy. As the NOMINALISTS put it, there is nothing in the *phenomenality* of things but that it is a feature of the NAMES we give to them. That is the shamanism of the foregrounded *figures* that we have learned to perceive in our looking-and-thinking world—learned so well that we take them unconsciously as matters of fact."

Roy: "Learned by matter-of-factly *discounting* the inherently confusing second-attention *background* of things and people. Which is, of course, RECTIFIED in the hyper-objective, inherently *pragmatic* lucid *waking* experience."

Coyote: "Hence the distinction drawn by the Amazonian peoples between the *daylight* shamans (Coyote's RAVENS, or *shamans of the Essences*), and the *night* shamans (RAVEN'S coyotes) of the dreaming-vision sort. Night shamans have the body | within the spirit-vision, while daylight shamans have the spirit-vision within the physical body and figure their version of the inner dream within the contortions and movements of the body itself—catalepsy."

Roy: "*Sonnets* are waking-visions of the sorcerer's catalepsy, shaking it all out in the rhythmic conceits of rhyme-scheme and AUTOMIMETIC voice—the Shakespeare-seizure."

Coyote: "And the *Caesura*. The Siberian shamans, according to ANNALEINA SIIKALA, also make this distinction; they say that the cataleptic body-dance, as EDIE TURNER calls it, is simply another form of shamanism."

Roy: "Then the ANTI-TWINS, *DIE GEGENZWILLINGEN* (why do these things sound so *satisfying* in German?), would be the form of anti-cataleptic seizure by which the human race itself came into existence."

Coyote: "Systole and diastole, out-breath and in-breath. The in-your-face METABREATH, the turning of the world, as in the *Prologue* to Goethe's *Faust*: '*Es wechselt Paradieses Helle / mit tiefer, schauervolle Nacht.*' 'It changes—paradise—illumination with deep, shuddering night.'"

Roy: "Green, the midpoint of the RAINBOW, was Goethe's favorite color. 'That color,' he said in the *Farbenlehre*, 'in whose presence you wish to be nowhere else.'"

Coyote: "And it was also, apparently, that of the Mayans, as exhibited in the magnificent Quetzal that illuminates the twilight of the deep forest."

Roy: "Whereas Don Juan knew the assemblage-point cohesion of the *crow* position, and could actually turn himself into a crow:

The quetzal and the crow, their colors vary
from iridescent green to black withal,
refraction clouds its spectrum in their caul;
there are no words in twilight's dictionary
but diagrams of darkness standing tall,
unfazed by sunlight, vocable, contrary,
that crack the code of time's vocabulary—
at certain times there are no gods at all.

In certain moods the whims of mortals crack,
uncertain of their lives and what they mean,
like wings of crows that bring the shadows back;
then suddenly, that incandescent GREEN
unspeakable, that takes the light aback—
at certain times the shadows split the scene."

The ANTI-TWINS, Again and Again

Coyote: "At certain times all the permutations and combinations of ordinary TWINNING are not enough, and ANTI-TWIN-NING must come to our rescue, given that the human part of any animal enterprise is also the animal part of any human enterprise."

Roy: "All the powers in the knowable universe, from the micro-fauna to the slowly turning galaxies, are *animal powers* and dispensations of our own special symmetry, if only because it takes *our* symmetry to know what symmetry is, and our animality to know what existence is."

Coyote: "The twinning *outward* of the bodies into two separate genders is a thing we share with most 'higher' forms of organization in living creatures. The twinning *inward* of those bodies into the single individual, with the right and left side laterality, is likewise a thing we share with those creatures."

Roy: "Other creatures probably tell stories and even *jokes* in ways that we cannot fathom, particularly *cats*, but there is one way in which human beings may be unique, and that is in the comprehensive knowledge of TWINNING as a living symmetry in its own right."

Coyote: "Although other creatures have their own ways of dealing with this, possibly superior to our own, the *comprehensive* knowledge of TWINNING for human beings goes both ways at once, both positive and negative, inside and outside."

Roy: "They, the ANTI-TWINS, are the *gender symmetries*. We are the laterality symmetries. *They* have only one side each, which is why they are practically invisible, but each of them has *both* genders. We have only one gender each, which is why we are *impractically* co-dependent, but each of us has two sides. Because *sides* reproduce themselves technologically, *we* are necessary to create them, but because genders reproduce themselves corporeally we are at their mercy in matters of love, personal choice, and mating. They have the *shoulders* for gender-choice, but we have the shoulders for alterity, for 'yes' and 'no.'"

Coyote: "You mean when *we* fall in love it is really *them*?"

Roy: "Yup, and when *they* fall into anonymity it is really *us*."

Coyote: "It is only through our misconception of them that we can truly be, and only through their misconception of us that their otherwise invisible presence comes into relief. It's like each is the negative of the other's photograph. They come together as we fall apart and vice-versa, and by virtue of this invisible counterpoint, both gender and laterality come *full circle* for the species that has a full knowledge of them.'"

Roy: "In a fully *conscious* and *deliberate* way, by turns, as in the systole and diastole of breathing. We EXPERSONATE them as they impersonate us, and they EXPERSONATE us as we impersonate them. *Gender* closed inward upon itself is INCEST, Coyote, a thing we are all trained to avoid. And *laterality* closed outward upon itself is *technology*, the central spinal hinge of the body placed outside of the body in the realm of the positive doing and thinking of things."

Coyote: "So, we have made a great mistake in our thinking of reproduction, and in telling stories about the birds and the bees."

Roy: "What is truly active in reproduction, what Shakespeare called 'the beast with two backs,' is not the man and the woman as we normally fancy them, but two unlikely counterparts: *the male part of the woman and the female part of the man,* the ANTI-TWINNING counterparts of our normal gender specifications. With a nod to Shakespeare we may call this 'equipositioning':

Making the Back with Two Beasts

At either end a countenance appears,
a social face, anonymous inside
where all is one, and conduits decide
(perception dulls the mind, conception clears)
that somewhere in its past our language lied,
tongue matching tongue, the posture in arrears
(the sidelong glance, the conduit, interferes);
inequus taught his mistress how to ride.

The necks entwined, the tails eject like sperm
or flags that fly and need no further glory,
the sweat of detumescence drinks the loins.
"There are no separate bodies," life enjoins,
"no loves but those liquidities confirm,
like conduits matching conduits, *con amore.*"

Coyote: "So, Roy, is the sonnet the veridical ANTI-TWIN of language?"

Roy: "In a manner of *coupling*, yes, otherwise you may think of them as Mother Nature's crossword puzzles. They are *hybrids*, like months that happen in between seasons, or artifacts that belong to neither nature nor culture, as Bruno Latour points out in *We Have Never Been Modern*. Our civilization at this point is incapable of producing either a purely uncontaminated description of the natural or a a technological product that is not in some way a coyote imitation of the natural—an auto-*mation*."

Coyote: "You humans wouldn't notice, but deer and horses have almost the same *scent*."

Late October, "Deerback"

More serious than snow, the rank and file
of deer, their long coats darkened, face to face
with procreation's hoodwink of the chase
make pace to consummate, to mate with style.
And something old as treetrunks has the grace
to banter with the crimson solar smile
and have the deadened crickets wait a while
amid the smoke and what the trees erase.

We call this half-month "deer bark" for the cough
that bucks presume, as though, to scorn a snare
the silhouetted wind were sounding off
unkindly. "Tell me love is never fair,
the times that most engage us never free,
joy has no counterpart in ecstasy."

Roy: "What Latour did not point out is that this inability to either comprehend or fabricate the spontaneity of what we call "nature," or the self-imitation of what we call "culture," *goes all the way through* and infects the very species that would like to 'purify' itself through such symbolic sleight-of-mind."

Coyote: "You are talking about Soccer Mom and Corporate Dad, the twenty-first century falsifications of what used to be called the middle-class couple."

Roy: "Sure, the male whose masculinity cannot be acknowledged without submerging it in a kind of Group Voice Group Action charade of what an executive used to do and the woman whose maternity cannot be acknowledged without the ad hoc inclusion of a sports team."

Coyote: "I get it. In an age where *products* work hard to produce *people* (or else what are all the advertisements about?), what is left for the people to do but reproduce cross-products, a hybridized version of what reproduction was supposed to mean? Metrosexuals."

Roy: "They eat exclusively organic food, believe in exclusively inorganic robots, and live in electronic co-dependency with photonic people who might just as well not be there."

Coyote: "Look, Mr. Wise Guy, if the ANTI-TWINS are as well nigh *universal* as you say they are—the "other half" of the human race as necessary for our survival as we are to theirs—then they must have worked this double-or-nothing dumbout magic all through the ages, *substitution* being one of the oldest things in the book."

Roy: "But not *electronically* or on a *global* scale:

Cell Phone Monkey Voice God

The tapestry of voices making small
unconversations, substitutes for facts;
there is no world behind its artifacts,
no other-voice convergence after all.
Like echoes miming all that air subtracts
in die-electric accents that appall
unwittingly, electrons make their call
in liquid silver lightning cataracts.

The succulence of fruit before the rot
just hangs around to make you wonder how,
like senior citizens at Angkor Wat
or fruit flies, or the bugs around a cow;

all cultures are invented on the spot,
I'll bet you think they're people, don't you now?"

Coyote: "Boy, Roy, wouldn't Oswald Spengler feel deflated to think
that his favorite *Faustian* culture—you know, the one that sold
its soul to the Devil in return for POWER (and keeps repeatedly
doing so, nothing like *persistence*, eh?)—would wind up figuring
out the secret of every civilization but its own?"

Roy: "Give the man a break, Coyote. He died under house-arrest
by the Nazis after trying to get the Pope to excommunicate Hitler and forestall a German-Italian alliance."

Coyote: "Whereas Joan of Arc, Spengler's ANTI-TWIN in
several respects, died in a much worse way, but wound up
with the Pope's blessing—a *battlefield promotion*, no less, to
SAINTHOOD!

Roy: "She could as well have been a Greek oracle, or a Roman
sibyl, or . . .

Jeanne D'arc Re-Envisioned as a Mayan Princess

Presume that mating's matings are a must,
now spring befalls the fall in double time,
the sacrament of slime begetting slime
bespells allotted ends like fairy dust
containing decontainment, *make it rhyme*,
now pollen shingles evergreens with rust
and stallions with their heavy necks downthrust
bleed power through the earth like slaking lime.

We have these other lives, like anti-twins:
the one that only thinks it acts, reflection,
the other acts so well it never thinks
and never has to, missing the connection
like gods of other lands exchanging winks
or, in the Mayan context, wicked grins."

Coyote: "But why so *particular*, Roy? Why so many *sonnets*? It
looks like someone is *showing off*."

Roy: "Warriors do not show off, Coyote. they *show brave.* And as to *particulars,* who would want to live in a universe of broad, shallow generalities? 'Empty idealities,' as Don Juan called them. Besides, did you ever stop to think of what the world would look like from the standpoint of the sonnet?"

Coyote: "You talk as if there were only *one* sonnet."

Roy: "Sure is, that's what we mean by *the sonnet.* There is only *one* real sonnet, just as there is only one real non-pair of ANTI-TWINS, plus, of course, a whole lot of cheap imitation "wannabes." All the most practiced sonneteers keep trying to get that one sonnet down in a purely objectifiable form, and the result is a plethora of sonnets like you wouldn't believe. All the lovers in the world keep trying to get the ANTI-TWINS down in a purely subjectifiable form, and the result is a lot of mistaken identities. A whole world full of them."

Coyote: "Whereas, of course, the one true sonnet is both amused and exasperated by all the fuss made about it. It is the absolute and most concise condensation of incredible richness and purposeful acuity of all the possible *meaningfulness* that could exist in the universe."

Roy: "Wow, Coyote, you sometimes surprise me!"

Coyote: "Beauty kills!"

Roy: "But the best way of killing, as the Native Americans say, is to *kill 'em with kindness.*"

Coyote: "And that's what God tried to do, at the first moment of Creation: He created the perfect ANTI-SONNET, which we know of as the matter and energy cosmos."

Roy: "You mean like the German physicist Lichtenberg said, 'Man created God in his own image'?"

Coyote: "Don't be silly, Roy; that was just the Enlightenment talking. I mean like, 'In the beginning the IMAGE created both Man and God together in its own sweet time.'"

Roy: "And then a strange, bearded figure appeared out of the background radiation of the Big Bang and said, 'LET THERE BE LICHTENBERG.'"

Coyote: "You just don't get it, do you, Roy?"

Roy: "I sure do. *The perfect sonnet must be in equilibrium with the rest of the universe in exactly the same way as it is in equilibrium with itself.* Thus, in a strange 'kill 'em with beauty' way, it becomes a scale model *miniature* of the universe, but much more perfect than the original."

Coyote: "So how does that square with your definition of Anthropology as the one discipline above all others that trains its students to perceive originality, be alert to originality, define it, codify it, objectify it, and then use it as a weapon against their otherwise derivative colleagues"?"

Roy: "Exponentially."

Coyote: "Well then Mr. Kill 'Em With Kindness, I've got, as they say in the trade, a BIG SURPRISE for you:

The Anthropologist

Most anthro-people live by poetry
too much, in fact, to do their writing good,
they know a thing much better than they should,
no heart for loss, no time for victory.
The 'cultural' are barely understood,
the 'social' ones make do with apathy,
'historical,' they have no history,
the excavator's fame is made of wood.

Most anthro-people work without a muse
and make their near relations wonder why;
if arrogance were bliss they'd win a prize—
the editor that cuts them down to size—
Oh save their sorry asses from reviews,
God help the place they go to when they die."

Roy: "Story of my life."

Coyote: "Yeah, in *your* terms. You and all the other self-important narcissists."

Roy: "So what, in *your* terms, is this *creation* stuff, this ANTI-SONNET, all about?"

Coyote: "Well, I'd better use Albert Einstein's terms or I'll get the physicists on my back."

Roy: "Very few physicists, Coyote, have the guts to write a sonnet. I think Oppenheimer could have, before he was *disemboweled* by Mr. . . . how did he put it? . . . Strawz:

As when, in love, the same deft stroke bisects
the loins, and makes the man and woman groan
with equal passion differently, the tone
of bird and frog and cricket interjects
the twilight; laboring cicadas own
the embryo of sleep that brooks no sex
but breeds the firefly's art, and moss collects
its attitudes from molecules of stone.

Oh, listen to the night's acoustic blue
protracted conversation, monotone—
the nightbird's clock, alarm of katydid,
the catcalls of the owls, the forest's drone:
feel sorry for the ones that never do
a thing on earth, and for the ones that did."

Coyote: "*Einstein*, Roy, we were talking about Albert Einstein."

Roy: "You mean he had the guts to write a *sonnet*?"

Coyote: "Relatively speaking, no. But he had the *cat-guts* to play a violin. Besides which, he was one of the major articulators of what we could call the matter-energy universe."

Roy: "The ANTI-SONNET that was there at the beginning?"

Coyote: "Actually, it came into being in the roaring twenties, just before his confrontation with Niels Bohr; the time of Prohibition just before the Great Depression."

Roy: "Correct me if I'm wrong, but the major difference between a *material*, or matter-energy universe, and a *conceptual*, or order and chaos one, is one of *expansion* on the one hand and *meaningful condensation* or *verbal acuity* on the other. Like what they used to call 'the Fitzgerald contraction' in physics and 'plenty of speed but poor control' in the Charleston."

Coyote: "Are you referring to F. Scott Fitzgerald, the writer, or to another physicist of the same name?"

Roy: "Actually I am referring to Zelda Fitzgerald, F. Scott's wife. You see, it is all a matter of *obviation*, as we discussed earlier. A matter and energy cosmos, as Einstein pointed out, makes the equilibrium between matter and energy a function of celerity (c)and the velocity of light (electromagnetic emission), as in the equation $E = mc^2$. Such a cosmos *must* expand outward, since extension itself, or "space-time," as Einstein and Minkowski called it, depends for its existence on a velocity, a very large one."

Coyote: "You mean, 'getting out of Dodge?'"

Roy: "No, I mean getting *into* one, or at least, as Zelda would say, 'On the dodge.' You see, $E = mc^2$ is by definition a *quadratic* equation, based on a *squared quantity*, and a quadratic equation has *two possible solutions*, placing Einstein into *double jeopardy* as to the conformation and destiny of his matter and energy cosmos."

Coyote: "As Marilyn Monroe would say, 'His *roots* are showing.'

Double Jeopardy

The past is future's dandelion, lest
a single puff of air bestir its bubble,
expand its universe like Edwin Hubble,
control your breathing, keep your thoughts at rest.
Brunettes are prodigies at bending double,
the long division of the vision quest,
twice shriven, twice absolved, and twice confessed,
a blonde's the very nicest kind of trouble,

as dandelions go, a perfect gem
to force the spectrum into category,
decipher it, and code it into rhyme,
Diana, long of wit and long of stem,
but he who takes a redhead into glory
is prisoner of color, not of time.'

Always wondered about the 'red shift,' didn't you, Roy."

Roy: "Better than a *Doppelgänger*, Coyote. You see, as long as he could *rationalize* his choice of a *positive root* for the velocity of light, Einstein and his matter-energy cosmos were out of trouble. Then the universe would behave just exactly as the astrophysicists say it does, sending us messages in 'fossil light' from long dead quasars, supernovae, and galaxies (plus the occasional long-legged redhead) far out in the firmament."

Coyote: "But the minute he dropped his guard and intuited that his rationalizations were no more than pipe dreams, a wholly different cosmos revealed itself to him, one in which *he* would be the fossil and *it* would be a *delight*, based on the properties of the *negative velocity* of electromagnetic emission. In that case, space and time would play *inverse* roles to the ones we know and love so well; time would take on flesh and substance, as Mikhail Bakhtin pointed out, and space would become responsive to *it*. And of course, your redhead would give rise to one of her justly famous *45-minute-long chained orgasms*, with you hanging on to the bedframe to avoid being 'thrown.'"

Roy: "Ever wonder where those equine metaphors come from? The Russian literary critic and temporal philosopher Mikhail Bakhtin was the first human being to figure out what the inverse of Einstein's *space-time* would be like. He called it the *chronotope*, or 'time-space,' and said it was the definitive continuum for the shaping and staging of a literary work."

Coyote: "The perfect antidote to the matter and energy space-time ANTI-SONNET."

Roy: "Yet we know nothing of his passion for *horses*, first domesticated, they say, in southern Russia.

Equipoise

We use a kind of leverage, the face,
the elbow-joints and knees, the pantomime
emotions of the heart, to make sublime
the patterned movements that our thoughts erase,
to lift the tail and arch the neck of rhyme,

use equine sweep and figure to make pace—
the borrowed muscles of the human race
forget themselves as language every time.

To flay the teeth with pheromones, to mate
convolvular the long and rolling gait,
the rigid back that liquefies the leather;
to sound the eunuch-horn, to make the noun
re-verb-erate, to take the wind in tether—
what good is Poetry when written down?"

Coyote: "Or $E = mc^2$ either? Actually, if the equation is to have any
value at all, that is, to accurately describe the matter/energy flux
in the universe (the 'equipoise,' as you call it), it must be accept-
ed at face value. That is, the negative and positive values of the
velocity must be valid at the same time."

Roy: "There is both the *physical* fact of starlight as it moves
through the volumes of space and the *representational* fact of
starlight as it comes together in the formation of the equation.
Each of these requires a different vectoring of the stuff of the
matter-energy cosmos. The actual *phenomenon* observed by the
astronomer is a *hybrid*, just like you and me."

Coyote: "It is just as valid to conclude that we receive 'fossil light'
from distant objects out there in the firmament as it is to say:

**Starlight Grows Forever Younger as It
Ages the Cosmic Expanses around It**

Extension *is* expansion; we contract
(in subtle ways, when sonnets have their say—
this gives us fortitude, it gives us play)
the universe, our sullen artifact;
no conscious or subconscious blocks our way,
the foaming line intends the cataract
(you take the word for law, *we* take the fact)
extension *is* expansion, make my day!

But why the starlight moves a thousand ways
in manifold suspension, let you guess
(astronomers, astrologers confess
the infinite, remote, the end of days),
and why perfection's spectrum ends in blue,
You know exactly why, and always knew."

Roy: "Always *one thing in the context of another*, hey Coyote? Never any one thing by itself. Even a sonnet, like an equation, or, for that matter, the self-enclosed world of the laws of thermodynamics, must obey the fundamental axiom of self-reaction and must become an eternal prisoner of that least estimable part of ourselves: the recollecting self. Didn't anyone around here ever hear of *spontaneity*?"

Coyote: "Sure, Roy, that's the other kind of SYMMETRY, one-upmanship, the obverse twinning of twinning itself with ANTI-TWINNING, or what Don Juan calls "the ulterior configuration of the abstract.""

Roy: "Leibnitz's *Monadology* describes a perfectly self-enclosed perceptual universe for each individual, a world in which even *physical motion* is an illusion, like the famous "Holo-deck" on the starship Enterprise. Also like the two concurrent spatio-temporal motions necessary to validate the $E = mc^2$ equation, both backward and forward at once, *whereas the equation itself remains perfectly static the whole time*."

Coyote: "And like that lucid dream your teaching assistant Doug Elfers had about the motion inside of us in relation to that on the outside. Remember? In his dream, Doug saw what Don Juan calls an "ally" leaning against a sports car. The ally jerked its thumb at the sports car and said, "This thing is a *perception accelerator. By means of regular, mechanical motions, the car moves the assemblage-point of the driver to the place it will be at when the car arrives at its destination*.""

Roy: "Holy corroly, Coyote, do you know what THAT means? It means *anticipatory intelligence, first knowing, future memory*, and the true opposite of the merely recollective intelligence that our physics and our literary acumen exclusively depends on. It means what Don Juan calls 'the ulterior configuration of the abstract' and 'the somersault of thought into the impossible,' and what the Tenant in *The Art of Dreaming* calls 'flying backward and forward on the NOW energy of time.'"

Coyote: "Hey buddy, gimme a break. I don't even know what 'assemblage point' means, and as for sports cars, I usually *run* from them."

Roy: "Well, in this case, it means something like 'the anticipating self,' in Don Juan's teaching on the Double, you know, that part of our being or acting self that the recollecting self can never catch up with—the part that is always *gone* by the time you look for it."

Coyote: "Actually, I'm from Missouri—you gotta *show* me."

Roy: "Well, look: *everybody* is present at the point of their own conception, otherwise there would have *been* no conception, and therefore no *them*. 'You just had to be there,' as the saying goes. In that same way, the whole *universe* had to be there at its point of inception, or origin, but it stands to reason that neither you nor the universe could know what was going on at the time."

Coyote: "So, *knowing* you are at the point of conception is basically getting *screwed*, what the Bible calls 'carnal knowledge.'"

Roy: "Close, Coyote, but as Freud would say, 'no cigar.' There is another saying that is going to help us out a lot here, and fortunately it is a Jewish one: 'Just *knowing* is not enough, you gotta know *from* it.'"

Coyote: "So I wouldn't know my own conception until I had a *conception* of it, like a two-way holographic *orgasm* of myself, and the universe itself had no conception until Einstein wrote his famous equation."

Freud: "Give the mutt a SEE-gar."

Roy: "See? it is all a matter of *anticipatory intelligence*: first ya gotta *be* there, and then ya gotta *see* there. Coyote makes himself up all over again every time he has sex, and the universe comes into being once more every time someone figures out a new origin for it.

Coyote: "Actually, I suspect cats.

Cats Do, After All, Have Something to Do with Conception; The Only Question Is *What*

Be still, there is no absent source, no mother,
no afterbirth, Big Bang precipitate,
no child-support, behind-on-payments mate;
all sex implies a ratio, with the Other
made wholly in the self, inconsummate.
All light is made to lie, all voice to smother
that genitals but spit at one another,
and all we do in bed is masturbate.

The work of cats at night is yet unwritten,
and void-of-course conception without meter,
the cat-without-a-line presumes no rhyme
(you'd think they'd leave a note, at least a kitten);
no memory, no word, no worried reader
forgets them back into the shape of time."

Roy: "Ever watch a cat play with an object until it disappears, *knowing the whole time that it would disappear,* and then sit around for a long time disconsolate, wondering where it has gotten to?"

Coyote: "Yep. Duh!"

Roy: "Well, that was doing the same thing to you that Don Genaro was doing to Carlos when he disappeared his car. ('See, you dope, you look just like I do at this point—clueless.') The cat was testing your *anticipatory intelligence,* and of course it drew a blank. You ought to be ashamed of yourself. *Look ashamed!*"

Coyote (looks ashamed): "Actually, boss, I didn't follow a single one of your examples, and I cannot even imagine the one you are about to give me."

Roy: "Good, because that would be *predicting*, and predicting is a sure-fire *symptom* of a merely recollective intelligence—making the future dependent on the past."

Coyote: "Like un-predicting would be making the past dependent on the *future*? You're gonna show me how to do that?"

Roy: "Bet on it, Bozo! I am going to show you the secret of the *self-modeling series* in mathematics, the most familiar example we have of a future-dependent variable. Remember, Coyote? We have already reviewed its relation to the Golden Section and the problems of resonance."

Coyote: "Sure, the famous *Fibonacci numbers*, how could I forget? Let's see, the series begins: 0, 1, 2, 3, 5, 8, 13, or maybe just 1, 2, 3, 5, 8, 13. . . . Or else, you could start at some later point, like 8, for instance, and go 8, 13, 21, 34 . . . Frankly, I don't *know* where the series ought to begin. It seems totally arbitrary."

Roy: "There's where you're wrong, Coyote. It is completely *determined*, once you know the secret. And the secret is very simple: each successive member of the series is expressed as the sum of the two *previous* ones, so that technically you could begin the series *at any point* provided that rule is obeyed. In theory, you could begin with *any two numbers*, provided the third is their sum, and go from there, and, Fibonacci or not, it would still be a self-modeling series."

Coyote: "So you cannot *know* where the series begins until you get into it."

Roy: "Precisely. The algebraic formula is $n + 1 = n + (n-1)$, where the value of *n* is a function of what goes before and what comes after it."

Coyote: "I got it! It's like a *rabbit* watching its back-track, trying to figure out what comes next from what happened beforehand. Like, for instance, *me*, so that I don't be what happens next."

Roy: "Or, in other words, *anticipatory intelligence*. See, Rabbit is justly famous throughout the whole animal world for making a positive virtue of complete naïveté, its power of having no power at all, like the zero. As in the saying, "The moon is Rabbit's reflection in his own eye."

Coyote: "And also justly famous for *littering*. That is, its proverbial procreative powers: having children all over the place, which might be thought of as 'reflections' of the parents as they mate under the full moon on the high plains at night."

Roy: "Thus Rabbit is as intimately related to the Hindu goddess Kali, 'The Protector of Children,' as the Golden Section is to the Fibonacci series, or the 'golden sectioning' of the moon. For Kali "watches her back-track" too, like that mysterious quantity n in the Fibonacci formula, a function of what goes before and comes afterward. As the Black Goddess of Time, she stands at the Eternal Present, the intersection of synchrony and diachrony—the presence and the passing of time, striking down offenders with her immense *sakti* power.

Kali's Rainbow

She keeps so many moonbeams in her jar
reflection could not calculate its months,
nor Rabbit's children, coming all at once—
so many plangents on the same sitar
interpolate the passage of her dance.
The rabbit moon is Kali's avatar;
no metaphor is what it thinks you are
but that it take your word as happenstance

the way the shadow moves beneath the rabbit,
like Kali's other art of hoppening—
the moon above, the goddess down below;
all power flows from manic breach of habit:
all kinds of songs there are you cannot sing,
all kinds of ways there are you cannot go.

Kali is the *darsan* goddess of double vision and double conception. For her, there is no time interval between 'the original conception of the universe' and the present moment, *whenever that moment might be."*

Coyote: "She is also, by my reckoning, the goddess of *motivation."*

Roy: "How can you know that?"

Coyote: "By watching my back-track."

Roy: "I don't quite follow you."

Coyote: "That is my point. I don't see you coming from where I have just been. Like two steps forward and one step back, you know, like that mysterious n in the Fibonacci formula. Or the place where Kali stands."

Roy: "People always act on the dead certainty of what will happen in the future, even though, and *especially because*, they are quite uncertain about it. . . ."

Coyote: "Whereas the only place where you can be dead certain about anything is the here and now, the eternal present."

Roy: "But that is the only place where I have ever been uncertain about anything."

Coyote: "See, Roy, *motivation* is not only linked to Kali, the moon, and Rabbit, but to the Fibonacci series and obviation, which *is also a self-modeling series*. The first two substitutions in the obviation diagram, marked A and B, are like the first two numbers in the Fibonacci series: they are *future-dependent* variables (motivated from the future) because you can only know how and why they are the way they are when you get to the *third term*, marked C (synthesis) on the diagram."

Roy: "So, Prince Hamlet could only know why he had *acted himself mad* (A) after his very motive was countermanded by Polonius's "To thine own self be true" at B, and then engaged *other actors* to stage the "dumb show" at point 0, the synthesis, for Claudius's benefit, showing that *actions speak louder than words*."

Coyote: "Thus, even though he did not know what would happen in the future, and was terribly uncertain about it at the time, Hamlet's decision to "act himself mad" at A was *retroactively motivated* by the dumb show at C. But C is also the beginning of a new triad, like any other Fibonacci sum. So Hamlet's effort to "get the goods" on Claudius at C, followed by his inadvertent stabbing of Polonius at D (killing Laertes's father just as Claudius had killed his, reversing the roles), "sets up" Claudius's illicit compact with Laertes at E, and thus retroactively motivates the synthesis at C."

Roy: "I get the point. 'Farewell to yesterday's tomorrow'—the *present* happens, but only and always under the illusion that it was the past that was doing it all along. The *real* motivation *underdetermines* the uncertainties of the present moment, and one *divines* the shape of one's own *intention* in that ruse."

Coyote: "Sure, Roy. If you take the trouble to go back and look at the obviation diagram, figure 6, you will notice that the three points of *synthesis*, C, E, and A (both the beginning and the ending), form the apices of the *internal* triangle, and that the arrows (of implication) connecting these run *clockwise* around the inner perimeter of the diagram. Those three points motivate the *retroactive* ('backward in time') provocation of the plot."

Roy: "But only because the *forward* progression of the action in the drama is represented in the diagram as moving *counterclockwise* around the outer perimeter of the diagram, according to the larger triangle BDF, whose apices form the *anti-motivational* (or 'resistance to free will') structure of the drama."

Coyote: "In that sense, of course the *outer* triangle BDF corresponds to the traditional model of *determinism*, or what is called "fatalism"—prediction from the past in science and *predestination* in Calvinism. It's the idea that all things are determined from the past, or at least that the shape of the *event*, the 'happening of things,' forms a kind of inevitable resistance to the exercise of free will."

Roy: "But, of course, *Hamlet* shows that kind of determinist nonsense to be an illusion, though a *necessary* one, as it sets the stage (as triangle BDF 'sets the stage' for triangle ACE for the kind of *underdetermination* that allows free will, or the free spirit, to trap itself in its own devices. Two steps forward and one step back; the self-modeling series of human destiny."

Coyote: "Roy, are you familiar with the saying, 'Memory has nothing to do with the past; its only purpose is to rearrange the *future*'?"

Roy: "I ought to be, I made it up. It takes us, via the Kali two-step, back to our point of origin and forward to the vast holographic knowledge of India:

Himavant

As *having* is the antidote to *want*,
the past is what the future does to change,
as all we can remember takes us strange—
the passive periphrastic of 'enchant,'
and memory is like a mountain range
where sleeps the snow eternal, *Himavant*,
its vistas blue and changeless, hanging gaunt;
all pasts are what the future shall arrange.

Each point on the horizon holds a sky
as overwhelming as the blue above—
how manifold the hologram, existence!
How multiplex the concourse of the eye—
or is it but some fickle god of love
distributing the loneliness of distance?"

Coyote: "There is a big problem, Roy, with all accounts of the origin of anything—the creation of the universe, the origin of life,
consciousness, rational thought . . . "

Roy: "And that is because it is unable to account for what came
before it, and so must compromise itself by trying to be self-
contained, or *sui-generis*, the way Oedipus did when he murdered his father and married his own mother."

Coyote: "Well, *that too*, though '*Sui Generis*' sounds like 'The
Mother Of All Pigs,' but it is not the one I was thinking about.
Anything that takes matters into its own hands, like a suicide,
challenges the Creator, especially where life is concerned. But it
is also true that any account that attempts to explain the purely
phenomenal nature of the universe—its matter and energy, order
and chaos, atoms and molecules, even *life*—is obliged to take for
granted the very *consciousness* that allowed one to be aware of it
in the first place."

Roy: "Whereas, of course, any account that attempts to explain the
purely *numinal* awareness of things—what awareness or consciousness *is* in the first place (what they call the 'spirit' or Don

Juan's *nagual*)—is obliged to take for granted the *phenomenal* reality. You know, matter and energy and life and all that. That is the most *obvious* thing about our everyday experience of the world around us."

Coyote: "That explains exactly why the greatest thinkers and philosophers of *any* age—prodigies like Heraclitus, the Vedic Hindus, Lao Tse, Plato, Aristotle, Kant, Hegel, Wittgenstein—are able to achieve marvels in the realm of human thought yet *are unable to make a consummate statement of their own direction and purpose.*"

Roy: "They leave that for others. They *make excuses* and assume that it will be self-evident to the reader, *which it almost never is,* except in the case of sophists and fools. Even Nietzsche, one of the best, suffered from this kind of trauma:

Nietzsche's Migraine

The word denies its suicide in rhyme,
each metaphor a sympathetic blur
to salve the hurt of language as it were;
the night is long, the predator sublime,
unsheathed, the claws retract again to fur
(absolve the witness, nevermind the crime)
like Zarathustra's laughter, keeping time
(to what, besides itself, does pain refer?).

Compose yourself; the somber violin,
cat's second favorite form of suicide
(it takes a stroke to help the beast unwind),
without it take you out, will do you in.
How like a brain to think itself a mind?
How like a cat to think it even tried?"

Coyote: "Wrong *animal*, Roy. Perhaps Nietzsche's sneaking suspicion about cats was well founded (*dogs*, like Prussians, are far more obedient), and perhaps he was the victim of *keberebidi* sorcery, but in any case *something* made a mistake. Just as the dreaming body, or *nagual*, is the *figure-ground reversal* of the waking body, or *tonal*, so the echidna is the figure-ground reversal of the dreamer and the dreamed."

Roy: "What? Come again?"

Coyote: "Psychologists have experimentally determined that the echidna's 'intelligence' (perhaps more of a savoire faire) is *inexhaustible*. It appears the creature is incapable of making a distinction between conscious and subconscious, environment and individual, or, for that matter, one moment and the next. Furthermore, it appears that the echidna brain lacks a hippocampus, the seat of memory, so that instead of acting on recall or recollection, echidnas are doomed to proceed improvisatorily as it were, reinventing the whole world ('of experience') anew at every step, and *on raw intelligence alone—anticipatory* intelligence. They 'walk forever in the eternal daylight of the *now*,' and, as if that were not enough, they also *glow in the dark*."

Roy: "So you're saying that the echidna is the *antidote* to Nietzsche's migraine?"

Coyote: "Ah'm sayin' that the echidna is the antidote to the whole of phenomenal reality and all that it may inherit; that it not only knows, but *embodies* the figure-ground reversal that divides our world into two equal halves—*any* two equal halves. And that it could write a sonnet exponentially better than any of yours, and *in between the lines* of your own thoughts."

Roy: "Oh yeah? I gotta see it to disbelieve it."

Coyote: "Voila

Echidna

What time dares not to multiply, divides,
itself within itself, as though immortal;
interpolated instants form a portal—
infinity within—and therein hides
time's secret in disguise, the neo-cortal
indefinite echidna; faith abides
the salvage-yard of mirror suicides
but not the joke without its punch line (chortle)

and not the laugh without the joke, perforce,
the mirrored sky recedes from blue to blue,
the shape of wings that unremembers birds;
echidnas mate, and call it 'undercourse,'
too whimsical for reprimand, and too
(as we have seen) indefinite for words."

The One Thing I Keep Trying to Tell You and That You Keep Trying to Tell Me

Roy: "About what? About you and I, or about the sonnet, the Anti-twins, anticipatory intelligence, Kali, the echidna, Nietzsche, or the figure-ground reversal?"

Coyote: "*All* of them, all of the above. You see, Nietzsche was the foremost philosopher of his time, the one who had figured out his true direction and purpose. Though, by that time, Hegel was dead, and no one else had the ability at conceptual *synthesis* to know what he meant, much less believe him. He called it 'the eternal return,' and everybody thought he meant something like *reincarnation* on a personal or cultural level."

Roy: "Spengler asserted that each 'high culture' had its distinctive *conceptual soul*, a way of perceiving extension, though they all shared exactly the same cyclical format. And Spengler claimed he got his whole 'overview'—something like Don Juan's *see-ing*—from Nietzsche."

Coyote: "Nietzsche wrote, 'What is truth? A mobile army of met-aphors . . . ,' and that would have to mean that the essence of meaning in a metaphor referred back to the one who was think-ing it. You know, like the One in the mirror who steals your act of looking, but only to see *itself*."

Roy: "But not the echidna, who needs no prior knowledge of *any-thing*, not even of itself. The Daribi use its dormant body for their memory-erasure sorcery. Remember?"

Coyote: "Like the zero term, *stupor mundi* ('wonder of the world'), as the medievals would say, and closely related to Kali: 'No met-aphor is what it thinks you are / but that it take your word as happenstance.'"

Roy: "Sure. 'Metaphor is language's way of trying to figure out *what we mean by it*,' like, 'Who, me? Funny thing you should ask.'"

Coyote: "So metaphor, or what we would like to think of as 'meaning,' is the not-doing figure-ground reversal of language, just as technology is the figure-ground reversal of human intention and action, and the echidna is the figure-ground reversal of memory and all it implies—the entire library of texts, clay tablets, equations, recorded formulas, memory-clips, and back-to-the-beginning, think-it-up-all-over-again analytic procedures that every civilization relies upon."

Roy: "Thus, conceptual or 'analytic' sophistication for most people means taking the grounding metaphors or analogical underpinnings of their religion, art, and science both literally and figuratively, so that fact and fantasy confirm each other, as in the sonnet. All *facts* are bizarre departures from the norm; all *norms* are bizarre departures from the fact."

Coyote: "And that has the adverse effect of fixing the perception of a single individual, or a whole civilization, within a single figure-ground reversal matrix that will rule them their whole lives. What Don Juan calls 'the axis of perception' defines the comfort-zone of everyday life, human mental and physical routines. He calls it 'the here and there,' that which is proper and more familiar to us as against what is comparatively alien or *other*, given that all our words and significant concepts come in *pairs*, and that we use our very imaginations to hold the figure-ground reversal in place."

Roy: "But it is *we* who are like that, not the world around us which has figure-ground reversals of its own. Like that river called the Swift Run that used to flow by my house, and told me its name was:

Shadow-Walker

This current named itself so long ago
the memories have memories, the trace
of ancient waterfalls, the carapace

of shadows moving through a glass too slow
for eye to catch them or the light efface
the netherworlds of depth that liquids know
the trees of autumn blanching row on row,
the upright posture of the human race.

"I am not like you, do not live or think
as custom has us mate in different styles,
nor love in any pattern made by ink,
or colored figures that the sun beguiles
to fructify the water as they sink;
I have forgotten loves, and secret smiles."

Coyote: "*Babes in the woods*, Roy, shame on you! You were not
taught to think that way, much less feel that way. If challenged
to put it into words, you could only *reflect* upon it and never *go
with the flow*. It's a dam good thing you human beings invented
names, otherwise you would be *speechless!*"

Roy: "We are all slaves of the figure-ground reversal format we
were born to, and it rules our conceptual ability every day of our
lives. That is the whole challenge of what Don Juan calls 'power,' and what we call Coyote Anthropology and what Nietzsche
called *Die Ewige Wiederkunft*, or the eternal return. The being
that could teach itself to *take control* of that ability to ground
the figure and figure the ground—that is, to *underdetermine*
the play of perspectives that control our movement, orienta-
tion, and emotion in the world around us (what Aristotle called
'the active subject')—that being would have *no limitations of
any kind whatsoever*. Even the life/death figure-ground reversal
would invert upon itself. As I once put it in a sonnet, 'There are
no more excuses for existence . . . uncomplicated gods invented
distance.'"

Coyote: "So, the reverse perspectives in Byzantine paintings took
them *halfway there*, and the figure-ground reversal masterpieces of M. G. Escher advanced the viewer's control *by another
quarter-turn*."

Roy: "Why do you say that, Coyote?"

Coyote: "Because they only *demonstrate the possibilities*, like a sleight-of-hand performance, whereas if the viewer could fully incorporate the underdetermination of figure-ground reversal within their *sensorium*, as Aristotle might put it, there would be no need for objectification anymore. Nietzsche went mad in the end, more or less like Hamlet. The Byzantine perspectives fell victim to iconoclasty riots, and M. C. Escher emerged as the true heir of Jan Vermeer, the greatest of all Dutch interior painters. Figure-ground control was *hard work* for these Magians and Faustians."

Roy: "But it was easy for the ancient Mayans, who used *animal powers*, just as we do in our sonnets. Just as *Hamlet* dramatized Shakespeare's intuition of *anticipatory intelligence* (each of the three cross-cutting axes of an *obviation*—'to anticipate and dispose of'—is a figure-ground reversal in and of itself), so the jaguar, called *balam* by the Mayans, gave them the precept for the independent invention of the zero-term."

Coyote: "The not-doing figure-ground reversal of *number*, or as you like to think of it, *quantity*, an anticipatory mathematical anomaly invented, as far as we can tell, only twice in human history: once in ancient India and once in Mexico. Though something of a conundrum in it self, it enables *place value* systems in mathematics. As they say in India, 'Even the leopard has its *spots*.'"

Roy: "Sure, but look closely at the *jaguar's* spots. At first approximation, they look like our zero figure, enclosing an empty space. But on closer inspection they are more like Greek *omega* signs, meaning 'the end.' But in the final analysis, they look most like cowrie shells, which served the Mayans as their glyph for the zero, the nothing that was *really something*:

Balam
for George Mentore

Deny the gods, invent some better law,
gigantic feline essence of the owl!

He has the deeper throat, the darker scowl,
the jungle-shaking gutteral, the JAW.
When all the shades of night are crying fowl
he lights the lamps of jade and loosens craw,
the hunter that his victims never saw,
the JAGUAR, liquesces on the prowl.

They did not need their gods in olden times,
no matter what our evolution thinks,
but took his passion, redefining crimes
from glancing at his spots, from sudden fright
invented ZERO in the sudden night,
the scare that wasn't there, the missing lynx."

Coyote: "Well, Roy, the jaguar may have given the Mayans their
nothingness, as you say, but it was a Coyote who gave the Aztecs their *language*. Surely you will have heard of Nezuauacoyotl, 'Hungry Coyote,' the great Toltec poet who was also ruler of
a city-state:

In hungry times did Nezuauacoyotl
bespeak the slain, the truth of the *atlatl*,
the *slurrogate* of speech, the sly *coatl*,
the serpent of the word, the sacerdotal.
The Mayan language took away its rattle
and jazzy Aztec made it almost *total*,
the *tonal* of the times is anecdotal,
the *snake of language* takes the word to battle.

However deep the throat or dry the throttle
the Aztecs made an Empire epiglottal,
they made an age of copper show its mettle
and made persuasion sing like Aristotle;
the snake-in-talons brought them there to settle,
the Pope of mountains, Popocatepetl."

Roy: "It was just that same swift, sure control over an inner faculty that can only be objectified with great difficulty; the underdetermination of perspectival figure-ground reversal that continues to strike awe and wonder in archaeologists, Castanedans, and all those who would try to make sense of Meso-American civilization. Don Juan said that the pyramids of ancient Mexico were envisioned as 'gigantic not-doings' to help the warrior contemplate the full implications of the *second-attention*, that part of us that acts in advance of recollective conventionality—the *anticipatory intelligence* of the Mayan long-count."

Coyote: "The so-called Mayan calendar was actually the *temporal opposite* of anything we know by that term; it used *omens* to 'unpredict,' that is, to certify the *present* via shrewd observations anticipated from a phantom future position. In that sense, the whole layout and emphasis of Meso-American culture can be treated and understood as a gigantic manipulation of the axis of perception—a not-doing of all we are familiar with as modern times, socio-political agendas, science, technology, ethics, and social relationships. It was *the city upside-down*."

Roy: "Second-attention reality was the same thing in both cases: the fundamental thing that drives or motivates us as human beings and makes life worthwhile. But it takes an opposite form in the two civilizations. In our modern, right-side-up cities, the power of second-attention—the essence of *metaphor, meaning, love, sexual being, action*, and perhaps the nature of time itself—is treated as *necessary* but *incidental* to our true aims and goals. For us, sex, love, and reproduction belong to the *private sector*, our non-public lives. Music is a form of *entertainment*, and metaphor and insight serve as *hypotheses* or *heuristics* to aid in understanding the hard facts of science. For us, the second-attention is 'subjective' (that means soft and squishy and iffy) and of passing interest to the businessman or scientist. When 'persuasion' does not work and goodwill goes by the board, they use the *implicate imperative*, the electronic command-structure of the computer (wise in the way that Caesar was wise), to *intimidate* people into doing their jobs. (A modern democracy has no slaves and needs none.)"

Coyote: "For *them*, the Meso-Americans, in their upside-down cities, it was quite the reverse: they were not 'bleeding-heart liberals' but open heart *specialists*, devoted practitioners on the sacerdotal level of the famous one-way Aztec open-heart surgery. Aortal ventriloquists, TAKE HEART! For them, the cosmos was not made of spatial intervals, but *moments in time*—a kind of time that obeyed no distinctions between phenomenal levels, the so-called *natural* and *social* discriminations that mean so much to us. For them, the so-called calendar was dictionary, encyclopedia, almanac, and Bible all rolled into one."

Roy: "The joke that brings the library down! They used omens to *divine* (not define) future events and happenings. They unpredicted, used the *future* to forecast the *present* instead of using the past to estimate probable and improbable futures. We use facts, observations, and experiments to prove the way things always were and always will be. For us, the second-attention is and always will be the ultimate frontier of knowledge, something scarcely to be realized in *anyone's* lifetime. For them it was proof-positive of the sum of all knowledge as an achieved quantity and of the effective internalization of the underdetermined perceptual figure-ground reversal within the human psyche. Or, if you will, the subliminal obviation of the axis of perception."

Coyote: "So the 'city upside-down' belies comparison with the metropolitan aggregations of other high civilizations in that it was not only a *not-doing* inversion of the Greek *polis*, the Roman *urbs*, the Islamic *medina*, but a mere *disguise* for the fact that Meso-American civilization could orient its structures in any way it wanted to. The *not-doing* that shows they had perfectly incorporated the concept of not-doing."

Roy: "The comparison is not unlike that of Hegel's contrast between the two kinds of infinity: the *bad* infinity of the mathematicians, so remote that no one could ever count up to it, and the *good* infinity of the perfect proportion perfectly realized, like Georg Cantor's epigrammatic proofs of the transfinite numbers. Or the perfect moment, the one statement that says it all because it underdetermines all others, the perfect *sonnet*."

Coyote: "When Western thinkers try to make sense of the perfect underdetermination of things, they tend to *over-literalize*. Like the object of the Large Hadron Collider, the most expensive scientific project ever conceived. This is supposed to be something called 'the God particle,' a particle so small that it underdetermines all the physical laws of the universe, and so, in a de facto sense, *is* God."

Roy: "But when Meso-American adepts chose to depict the underdetermination of *their* universe, they did so in a way that was both over-funny and over-serious at once, like the way in which Don Juan and Don Genaro taught Carlos. Look at the famous *Dresden Codex*, currently on display in Vienna. The human figures depicted in the text are in fact Genaro-like *caricatures*, comical *impersonations* of what Mr. Average would look like while doing those things. But the scenes or situations in which they are acting are the most deadly serious ones that that culture could conceive. Don Juan equates the super-serious *ex-personations* with *impeccability, the ulterior configuration of the abstract*, and 'the way of the warrior.'"

Coyote: "They expressed what we would call a *metaphor* in terms of its *extremes* rather than its *means* (what a 'meta' is 'for,' so to speak). So the Nahuatl (Aztec) metaphor for metaphor itself was *in xochitl in cuicatl*, literally "flower and song" but figuratively, on its own scale, 'visual image and acoustical continuity,' meaning 'everything that takes place between these two extremes.'"

Roy: "Take, for instance, the marigold, honored as a mortuary flower both in pre-contact Mexico and pre-contact Austria."

Coyote: "I cannot even imagine pre-contact Austria."

Roy: "Nor should you. I have enough trouble with post-contact Austria.

Marigold

Do not in vengeance smite the butterfly,
the featherwork belies the feather-crafter
and marigold's the crown of human laughter.

Do not becloud the deadly crystal's eye,
do not deny the bat his morning rafter,
his shriek that makes decryption of the sky,
make mordant of the evening's purple dye,
the alcohol of love the morning after.

Do not pretend to know the Mayan heart,
contrive a metaphor of heart's defiance,
the ways of hemoglobin mask an art,
the calendar's astrologies a science;
the whims of sorcery are feather-light,
and soft the owl that does its job at night."

Coyote: "Sometimes the most beautiful symmetries are also the
most deadly."

Roy: "The code name for Hitler's dreadful Night of the Long
Knives was *kolibri*, the German word for 'hummingbird.'"

Coyote: "I have never yet heard anyone make proper sense of the
ancient Mayan honorific for hummingbird: *Lord of the Black
Sun of the Fifth World*."

Roy: "That is because solar eclipses are so rare. And besides, you
don't ever, ever want to provoke that awesome-but-dreadful (the
Germans would say *abscheulich*) micro-macro power to work
its scale-change magic on you. You know—one moment it is a
tiny loving heart, drinking joy from the morning glories, and in
a flash it turns inside-out into a tornado and *walks the land in
devastation.*

Lord of the Black Sun of the Fifth World

Invisible, shot through with eye and wing,
the flower-taker's heart, the gnat of light
that makes each thing its opposite, the right
that knows no left but makes the distance sing;
Dark Lord of Eclipse, Jeweler of Flight
and Masquerade of Color, BEAR THIS THING:
THE WORLD IS GONE, the sun puts on its ring
of gold and black, the land espouses night.

Reflect the dark obsidian heart of man
in blue cenotes going down, take height
for depth, reverse the heavy charge of earth,
Horizon-in-Your-Heart, the wind's delight,
re-weaver of the daylight's masterplan,
UNTANGLE DARKNESS — BRING THE SUN TO BIRTH!"

Out of This World

Coyote: "The fact that the sun and moon cut out equal-area circles
in the sky is no cosmic accident by a long shot, and the fact that
their mutual occlusion in the solar eclipse is so rare—the solar
corona, *the sun's luminous energy-aura*, shines forth upon the
firmament—gives a highly privileged point of vantage to the
earth and all its creatures."

Roy: "It is related to the symmetry of the earth, the moon, and the
sun; to the symmetry of all living creatures to one another and
to the earth itself; to the underdetermination of equilibrium, or
balance; and to the curious fact that Wittgenstein noted toward
the end of the *Tractatus* that 'the eye does not lie within its own
field of vision.'"

Coyote: "Beyond that, it is related to what Goethe called the
Erdgeist, the 'Earth-Spirit'" or super-consciousness of the globe
upon which we all dwell: the fact—well known to the ancient Mayans, the Chinese, and probably the people of Stone-
henge—that the Earth itself is a sentient being."

Roy: "One that is capable, according to Don Juan, of feeling and
expressing all the emotions that a human being could possibly
feel, *plus a great many more* that are hidden from our empathy
within the multiplex planes or levels of its consciousness."

Coyote: "It could see more colors in the RAINBOW than the rainbow itself could see.

Rainbow (Chel)

O feathered serpent of the atmosphere
some iridescent eagle drew your arc,

some agate-eyed pit viper lit the spark;
you make the heart feel happy to be here.
Uncoil the sun.' Stay sudden in the dark,
outplume the birds, go silent like the deer,
collect the scent of flowers and appear
surprisingly, make eyebrow's question mark.

Light's introspection matches Mayan art
in grinning upside-down the world below,
makes sacrifice of storm, and sometimes twins
the crescent fantasy where thought begins
its artificial intercourse; they start
from nowhere, end in chaos, steal the show."

Roy: "Edge of the sun in the edge of the storm: the fractal patterning of light and darkness, confirmation and doubt, turmoil and
tranquility. *The rainbow itself does not lie within its own field of
vision*—you have to have the sun at your back."

Coyote: And that, in turn, brings us to the most profound of all
Wittgenstein's insights, the gem of the *Tractatus*. The one that
makes sense of this whole book, the totality of human or animal
cultural experience, and the central question of all great religions: '*The meanings of this world must lie outside of this world.*'"

Roy: "Well, they sure as hell do a good job of lying *inside* of this
world, so why stop there?"

Coyote: "Ya gotta stop *somewhere*."

Roy: "Ready to call it quits, Coyote?"

Coyote: "Ready when you are . . . might as well head back to the
Big Sky Country:

West Texas

To be forgotten in the way things are
like history or lifetime, rearrange
perspective inside-out, to know the strange
as intimacy, close, the way a star
becomes two distances that looks exchange—

a single currency of near and far,
the empty dot that was a railroad car—
'here' to itself alone, like open range

unfenced by the horizon, anyplace,
dumbstruck and flattened down by too much sky.
Some animal or bird, I know not which,
reflects its cloudscapes in a vagrant ditch
unflattered by the wind along its face,
and infinite the color of its eye."